ANATOMY OF INNOCENCE

ANATOMY OF INNOCENCE

Testimonies of the Wrongfully Convicted

Edited by Laura Caldwell and Leslie S. Klinger

Introduction by Scott Turow and Barry Scheck

LIVERIGHT PUBLISHING CORPORATION

A Division of W. W. Norton & Company

Independent Publishers Since 1923

New York | London

CONTENTS

CONTENTS

vi

10.

STAYING ON TRACK:
SURVIVING INCARCERATION

11.

THE BLOODY YELLOW SHIRT:
OBTAINING HELP

12.

THE LONG WAIT: LEGAL APPEALS

13.

THE LAST BAD MORNING:
EXONERATION

14.

MOVING FORWARD: POSTRELEASE

15.
EVERY DAY IS A NEW BEGINNING: LIFE AFTER INNOCENCE

INTRODUCTION

THE ULTIMATE HORROR

by Scott Turow

I was a federal prosecutor for eight years, hired straight out of law school. At twenty-nine, in those days, I was a little bit older than the norm, but I still had a lot to learn—a process that began rapidly with the first case I tried.

It was a good "starter case," the prosecution of a woman—I'll call her Patricia—a hapless street person, who'd sold a stolen welfare check to an undercover Secret Service agent. The transaction had been witnessed by four other agents, who were conducting surveillance. Conviction seemed virtually automatic. Patricia, and her federal defender, were proceeding to trial, probably because the judge, Prentice H. Marshall, was a die-hard liberal who believed that the Constitution meant what it said when it gave every defendant a right to trial (a view that's been virtually outlawed by the Federal Sentencing Guidelines). So long as Patricia didn't lie on the witness stand, Judge Marshall wouldn't penalize her for putting the government to its proof.

In order to secure the indictment, one agent, I'll call him Al, had testified before the grand jury and recounted seeing Patricia deliver the stolen T-check. When I was talking with the other Secret Service personnel, trying to decide which of them should be called to the stand at trial, one of them—I'll call him Bob—mentioned casually that Al hadn't been working the day of the crime. I consulted the other agents, who had similar memories. I directed Al to check his records. It became apparent that the defendant had been indicted on the basis of false testimony.

Judge Marshall was a former criminal defense lawyer who was notoriously hard on the prosecution. Thus, I experienced, not for the last time, a gut-level reluctance to reveal to the defense what had happened. In a narrow reading of *Brady v. Maryland*, the relevant evidence might not have been discoverable. Al's boo-boo, after all, had nothing to do with the ultimate issue of the defendant's guilt, especially if I didn't put Al on the stand at trial. My supervisor at the time in the U.S. Attorney's Office, Jim Streicker, introduced me to the rule I urged others to follow years later when I became a supervisor myself: If it hurts to turn the evidence over, turn it over. The reason for your discomfort is because you sense the proof might somehow help the defense.

So I turned the evidence over. The defense lawyer made the most of it. But Judge Marshall was unimpressed. To the judge, who'd been around criminal courtrooms for decades, it was understandable how an agent could go into the grand jury, months after the events in question, and confuse one surveillance with another. Because hearsay is allowable in grand jury testimony, Judge Marshall knew that the indictment would have been returned just as swiftly if Al had simply testified about what the other agents had reported to him. The judge regarded this as an innocent mistake, a little careless, but not perjurious. What mattered most to Judge Marshall was that the government had admitted the error, rather than trying to paper it over with lies. Judge Marshall, as he made clear, had seen that happen, too.

With the defense motion to dismiss the indictment disposed of, Judge Marshall quickly convicted Patricia. Her sentence, if I remember correctly, was light, even though she had far from a clean criminal record.

It was years before I recognized the most important takeaway from the case. In the last two decades, Barry Scheck and Peter Neufeld and the Innocence Project they founded have pioneered the use of DNA evidence in the courtroom, and we have thus learned that innocent defendants have been convicted of odious crimes far more frequently than many of us might have chosen to believe. Wrongful convictions are the law's ultimate horror. Our vaunted truth-finding system is quite capable of delivering false results. The consequence is a Kafkaesque nightmare for the defendant, and moral confusion for those who rely on the criminal justice system to accurately discriminate between good and evil.

In many instances, the cases reported in this book stir not just confusion but outrage, because they describe law enforcers who became law breakers, cops and prosecutors who tried to catch bad guys by becoming bad guys themselves: cops who tortured; cops who lied; cops who concocted confessions, often by feeding the defendant facts and then claiming the accused knew those details on his own; prosecutors and police who hid exculpatory evidence and obstructed justice in the process.

But as awful as those instances are, they tend to distract us from the real lesson of my first case, which is how prone our supposedly foolproof system is to innocent errors. Oddly, when I entered the U.S. Attorney's Office in Chicago, I knew that the criminal justice system wasn't flawless, because one of my best friends in the office, Jeremy Margolis, had been through the deeply upsetting experience of convicting an innocent man. Seven eyewitnesses had identified the defendant as the person who'd taken a father and son hostage at gunpoint from a restaurant on Chicago's South Side. By the end of the trial, the FBI case agent felt a worm of doubt, reinvestigated the case and the defendant's alibi, and located the alibi witnesses. The innocent defendant was released, while the actual criminal—a dead ringer for the man convicted—was found, already incarcerated in the Indiana state penitentiary.

In those days, it seemed that the competence and professionalism of the federal agents I worked with were an ultimate fail-safe for the system. I—and everyone else I worked with—was unwilling to abandon the longtime belief that eyewitness testimony was the gold standard of evidence. What could be clearer? Someone who was at the scene of the crime comes to court to tell us exactly what she or he saw.

But it turns out that because crime is blessedly rare, none of us are experienced in dealing with the shock of horrific events. When you add the realities of racial bias and a segregated society where people are often seen first by color, we find, all too frequently, that the gold standard is not even tin. Many of the cases described in the following pages show us how often eyewitnesses are mistaken. Sometimes they were cajoled by police. Sometimes they had an ax to grind. And sometimes the witnesses just made a mistake, under the stress of a terrible event.

But that is the paramount lesson: even good people, even dedicated professionals within the system like Al, make mistakes, with horrible consequences for defendants. Certainly the most heartrending parts of this book are the reports of virtually every wrongfully convicted person about the horrors of prison—the fear, the regimentation, the often brutal conditions—and the psychic pain of knowing these punishments are not only undeserved but the result of a supposedly careful system for finding the truth.

There are no quick fixes. Certainly, the law's insistence on finality has too often been a bar on rectifying errors, and there must be much greater latitude in adjudicating innocence claims, even years later. And we also need to be rigid in applying the reasonable standard and in letting jurors know what it means. Not "probably." Not "a high likelihood." Not "good enough." It has to be a standard that holds in mind the possibility of good-faith errors, and requires well-corroborated proof that eliminates even the chance of unintended mistakes.

Wrongful convictions will always be a part of a justice system administered by human beings. But a consciousness of that fact is a solid first step to minimizing those tragic errors.

SCOTT TUROW is a writer and attorney. He is the author of ten best-selling works of fiction, including his first novel, *Presumed Innocent* (1987); its sequel, *Innocent* (2010); and his newest novel, *Identical* (2013). His works of nonfiction include *One L* (1977), about his experience as a law student, and *Ultimate Punishment* (2003), a reflection on the death penalty. From 1978 to 1986, he was an assistant United States attorney in Chicago and served as lead counsel in a number of prosecutions related to Operation Greylord, a federal investigation of corruption in the Illinois judiciary. Turow has been active in a number of charitable causes including organizations that promote literacy, education and legal rights, and served as one of the fourteen members of the commission appointed in March 2000 by Illinois governor George Ryan to consider reform of the capital punishment system.

INTRODUCTION

THE UNREAL DREAM

by Barry Scheck

My colleagues at the Innocence Project and I have worked on close to 200 cases (193 to be precise, as this is written) involving innocent people wrongly convicted and then exonerated. I know well many of the hundreds of others who were exonerated by organizations in the Innocence Network.[1] These exonerees are truly special people. Each of them did not merely survive, they prevailed; each of them achieved a spiritual transcendence (not necessarily religious) that allowed them to avoid being consumed by hatred and bitterness. I recognize and greatly admire that process. But no matter how hard I try, no matter how many exonerations I attend, no matter how many exonerees I get to know, I cannot fully imagine nor understand their journeys.

---

1   The Innocence Network is an affiliation of more than sixty-five legal organizations around the nation and abroad that work to exonerate and assist the wrongfully convicted.

Sixteen years ago, in our introduction to *Actual Innocence,* Jim Dwyer, Peter Neufeld and I quoted Justice Learned Hand's observation in 1923 that "our procedure has always been haunted by the ghost of the innocent man convicted. It is an unreal dream." We noted then that those "ghosts now walk the land," but the "unreal dreams" lived by the exonerated were not yet being "counted" or adequately analyzed as to what went wrong and how it could be remedied.

Since then, due in no small measure to the efforts of people like my friend Scott Turow, who has litigated exoneration cases and written powerful studies and novels about the issue, more attention is being paid to exonerees, their cases and the aftermath. Scholars from many disciplines, innocence organizations, police and prosecutors are collecting data and trying to address root causes and remedies for wrongful convictions. There is a considerable body of academic literature that is sometimes called "innocence studies" that approaches the problem from all angles, including experts in organizational theory and cognitive science. There have been "sentinel event" reviews of wrongful convictions that involve "all stakeholders" and attempt to take a nonblaming "organizational accident" approach. There have been first-rate documentaries and feature films. A number of exonerees have written some very fine autobiographies.

But still, the most elusive problem, the most challenging aspect of the innocence narrative, remains truly comprehending the "unreal dream" of being wrongly convicted and imprisoned. It is a fear that drills into the marrow of our humanity, a nightmare from which each of the exonerated is trying to awake.

It is for this reason that *Anatomy of Innocence* is a welcome and unique addition to the field. Laura Caldwell—herself an innocence pioneer, having brought considerable attention to postexoneration issues—together with Leslie S. Klinger have shrewdly asked some great writers of mysteries and scripts for movies and television to focus on just a part of an exoneree's "as told to" experience, in a nonfiction fictional format. It forces these masters of compression and revealing observation to engage in a short-form exercise that Norman Mailer pioneered in longer form in *The Executioner's Song* and *Armies of the Night*, the novelist as nonfiction narrator.

It works surprisingly well—from S. J. Rozan's description of the eight hours that catapulted Gloria Killian from everyday law student to a perp-walking, accused murderer to Sara Paretsky's gut-wrenching evocation of the fear induced by Doty Road and unflinching moment-by-moment description of torture by police interrogators; from Lee Child's ironic observation that Kirk Bloodsworth could have avoided a death sentence by obeying an admonition from a fortune cookie to Laurie R. King's heartbreakingly intimate account of a judge privately urging Ray Towler to plead guilty.

There's Brad Parks's rendering of the agony of a juror

who tried to hold out before voting to convict an innocent Michael Evans to John Sheldon and Gayle Lynds's
take on the humiliation Audrey Edmunds endured while
endlessly trying to clear her name; from John Mankiewicz
capturing Jerry Miller's instant transformation from sex
offender to media star on the day of his exoneration to
Phillip M. Margolin drawing on his vast experience as a
litigator to describe the profound experience of William
Dillon becoming his own counsel.

From Jan Burke recounting Alton Logan's long days
in solitary to Sarah Weinman crawling inside the mind
of Ginny Lefever to describe her struggle that so many
people in every walk of life experience, how to not use
food as a crutch; from Jamie Freveletti's compelling coverage of the exoneration of Antione Day, which is both
heartbreaking and filled with hope, to Michael Harvey,
a lawyer, journalist and Academy Award–winning docu-
mentarian, delivering a visceral punch the first time Ken
Wyniemko walks into prison.

From Gary Phillips chronicling Jeff Deskovic's travails
through the New York court system to Laura Caldwell's
heartrending account of Juan Rivera, who greets the sunrise each day not just thinking of his little girl and his
family but also of the tragedy of a little girl and her family
to whom is he always connected.

Fittingly, the hitherto-unknown gem in this collection comes from one of the greatest writers of our time,
playwright Arthur Miller. In seven succinct, sledgeham-

mer paragraphs, titled "Luck and the Death Penalty," Miller describes how the conservative community of Litchfield, Connecticut, began to wonder whether they had wrongly convicted Peter Reilly in 1973 of raping, beating and murdering his mother based on the teenager's questionable confession to police. As the community raised money for better lawyers (Miller leaves out his own pivotal role as Reilly's advocate), Reilly's innocence is ultimately established in a postconviction hearing because the original prosecutor literally dropped dead on a golf course. A new prosecutor is appointed, who discovers in the state's file an undisclosed statement from a police officer demonstrating conclusively that Reilly was somewhere else at the time of his mother's murder.

Miller sums it up simply:

> The boy, Peter Reilly, regained his freedom in Litchfield County because a prosecutor died at the propitious time and because his neighbors believed in him, and outsiders were moved to come to his aid. The life of the innocent cannot be allowed to depend on that much luck nor the states dishonored by the pretentions of infallibility in absolutely every capital case that comes before its all but overwhelmed courts.

These words have as much or more force today as the day they were written. They bring into focus an irony that runs through all of these stories. Each exoneree profiled here is among the luckiest unlucky person you will ever meet. After reading Miller's essay, and after reading the "up close and personal" renderings of exoneree experiences by America's foremost masters of mystery, one conclusion is inescapable, although I strongly suspect it was not the avowed purpose of the contributors (with the exception of Miller)—America must end the death penalty to avoid the execution of the innocent. Our honor and moral core as a nation depends upon it. For that reason, and many others, we ought to be profoundly grateful to all the artists who contributed to *Anatomy of Innocence* and the exonerees who shared their stories.

BARRY SCHECK's more than thirty-five years of trial successes have earned him a national reputation. Scheck's criminal and civil trials have redefined and expanded the rights of victims of police misconduct and wrongful convictions throughout the United States. In addition to his private practice focusing on civil rights, Scheck cofounded and codirects the Innocence Project at the Benjamin N. Cardozo School of Law with Peter Neufeld. The Innocence Project has been responsible in whole or in part for exonerating most of the over three hundred men and women to be cleared through post-conviction DNA testing. Scheck is also a professor of law at the Benjamin N. Cardozo School of Law; in his more than thirty years on the Cardozo faculty, he has served as the director of Clinical Education, codirector of the Trial

Advocacy Programs and codirector of the Jacob Burns Center for the Study of Law and Ethics. Scheck is a past president of the National Association of Criminal Defense Lawyers. In 2000, he coedited, with Jim Dwyer and Peter Neufeld, the seminal book *Actual Innocence: Five Days to Execution, and Other Dispatches From the Wrongly Convicted*, and in 2003, he, Neufeld and Taryn Simon coedited *The Innocents*.

FOREWORD

by Laura Caldwell and Leslie S. Klinger

Civilization has struggled with the problem of guilt and innocence throughout history. In early days, guilt was determined by one or more deities, relieving humans of the burden of uncertainty, though even a god-based justice system had the fundamental problem of interpretation of ambiguous divine messages. Once humankind assumed the role of judge and jury, errors were inevitable. The legal principles on which the U.S. justice system is based recognized this, and for centuries, William Blackstone's principle, "It is better that ten guilty persons escape than that one innocent suffer"[1] prevailed, with a presumption of innocence and a standard of evidence of guilt "beyond a reasonable doubt."

---

1   English jurist William Blackstone expressed this sentiment in his seminal work *Commentaries on the Laws of England*, published in the 1760s. The principle has biblical origins: cf. God's reluctance to destroy the city of Sodom if even ten righteous persons could be found there (Genesis 18:23–32).

Although scholars have cast doubt on many supposed pillars of justice—such as in studies discrediting eyewitness testimony—for decades, the common view was that the U.S. justice system was virtually foolproof. The sentiment was perhaps most strongly expressed by a prosecutor who said in 1932, "Innocent men are never convicted. Don't worry about it. . . . It is a physical impossibility."[2] Justice Sandra Day O'Connor, in a 1993 concurring opinion in the U.S. Supreme Court's decision in *Herrera v. Collins*, wrote, "Our society has a high degree of confidence in its criminal trials, in no small part because the Constitution offers unparalleled protections against convicting the innocent."[3]

With the development of DNA-testing technology in the mid-1980s, that sentiment began to erode again. In 1989, two convicted felons were exonerated by postconviction DNA testing.[4] A third followed in 1990, with two more in 1991. As more exonerations occurred through means other than DNA, such as the discovery of new evidence, recantations or flawed science, the perception began to develop that the rate of error in the system was far greater than suspected. As

---

2   Quoted in Edwin M. Borchard with E. Russell Lutz, *Convicting the Innocent: Errors of Criminal Justice*, vii (1970).

3   *Herrera v. Collins*, 506 U.S. 390, 420 (1993) (J. O'Connor, concurring).

4   The exonerees were Gary Dotson and David Vasquez. See www .innocenceproject.org/cases/david-vasquez.

innocence consciousness grew, organizations devoted to exonerating the wrongly convicted came into being along with the word "exoneree"—someone who was factually innocent, wrongfully convicted and eventually exonerated.

The first American organization focused on exonerations was Centurion Ministries in Princeton, New Jersey, founded in 1983. Soon thereafter attorneys Barry Scheck and Peter Neufeld established the Innocence Project in New York City, which began using DNA testing to prove innocence. Their highly influential book *Actual Innocence* (2000) called for the creation of similar innocence organizations at law schools around the country. By the time of publication, the idea had already germinated, and innocence organizations had sprung up in the states of Washington, Wisconsin, Arizona, Illinois and California. By the early 2000s, these projects organized an innocence network to facilitate the sharing of information and support for the movement. As of 2016, the Innocence Network included sixty-nine members in virtually every state in America as well as Argentina, Australia, Canada, Ireland, Israel, Italy, the Netherlands, New Zealand, Taiwan and the United Kingdom. Perhaps even more importantly, as public awareness of wrongful convictions grew, by reason of prominent stories such as that of American exchange student Amanda Knox and large audiences for documentaries such as NPR's podcast *Serial* and Netflix's

Making a Murderer, many prosecutors' offices around the United States began creating conviction review units, using outside-the-office opinions, to examine cases of those who claim innocence.[5]

As the number of exonerees grew, another problem became apparent: after-innocence support. Coeditor Laura Caldwell explains how she came to found Life After Innocence, an organization that strives to provide or connect exonerees with record expungements, declarations of innocence and legislative support, and partners with organizations assisting with housing, employment and education.

"In 2008 law students approached me and suggested we start an innocence organization. I had previously represented a nineteen-year-old charged with murder who was in county lockup for six long years prior to his trial, and I'd written a book about the case (*Long Way Home: A Young Man Lost in the System and the Two Women Who Found Him*). Upon hearing the suggestion for a new innocence organization, I did what any lawyer does—research.

"I read about the innocence movement, and I reached out to some of its leaders, like Rob Warden and Karen Daniel at the Center on Wrongful Convictions and Barry

---

5   For example, www.dailynews.com/general-news/20150704/
la-county-da-creates-a-wrongful-conviction-unit. According
to the 2015 report of the National Registry of Exonerations
(http://www.law.umich.edu/special/exoneration/Documents/
Exonerations_in_2015.pdf), there were twenty-four "conviction integrity units" in 2015, quadruple the number that existed
in 2011.

Scheck and Peter Neufeld at the Innocence Project. I learned that as busy as they were fighting to get innocent people out of jail, they were also working very hard to help them start over.

"Both organizations soon added social workers to their staff, but many other innocence organizations were fiscally unable to do so, given the nature of their missions and certain grant-funding requirements. Eventually, the students at my school and I decided to create Life After Innocence."

Culturally, we are much more aware today that wrongful convictions happen frequently. Some estimates say as many as 5 to 10 percent of the prison population may be wrongly convicted persons, which leads to a potential number of 200,000 people who are innocent and in prison today. Yet very few understand *how* wrongful convictions happen, why they happen or how some could have endured the experience. Even more importantly, though the statistical dimensions of the problem are significant, the stories told here make clear that the personal costs of wrongful convictions are beyond counting.

As successful as Life After Innocence and other projects are in their efforts to help exonerees, they realize their absolute inability to address the trauma or to provide consistent support, and they know they've only scratched the surface of the vast needs of exonerees.

Imagine, for example, that two men have spent the same twenty years inside a state prison system. The men went in on the same day and were released on the same day. Imagine one of those men has admitted the crime and is a rightfully convicted murderer. Imagine the other is innocent and was wrongfully convicted of murder. Those men, upon being released, are often entitled to very different things. Traditionally, the rightfully convicted ex-offender is entitled to *much* more from the state than the innocent person (although sadly not much at all). Why is that true? Because exonerations, in Caldwell's words, are "the once-dirty little secret of the criminal justice world."

Chapter-by-chapter, this book illustrates how innocence can be thwarted and eventually may be regained. To add power to the voices of these exemplary exonerees, we asked highly skilled mystery and thriller writers— all students of the criminal justice system and how it affects those caught up in it—to tell the exonerees' stories. Writers have long aligned with causes. In the late nineteenth century, Émile Zola stood up for Captain Alfred Dreyfus. Later, Arthur Conan Doyle championed George Edalji, Oscar Slater and Sir Roger Casement. In the 1950s, Erle Stanley Gardner, the creator of *Perry Mason*, created the "Court of Last Resort" to take up the cases of those whom the justice system had failed. Later, writers like Arthur Miller (whose previously unpublished essay is included in this volume) and Norman Mailer fought for justice for wrongly accused individuals. It was only natural, then, to pair contemporary master storytellers with exonerees for this book.

Anatomy of Innocence presents wrongful convictions and exonerations as a collective national experience, examined from a variety of perspectives. *Anatomy* tells the incredibly true stories of fifteen innocent men and women and reveals the intense emotions they experienced during their journey to exoneration. In the end, *Anatomy of Innocence* is unique in examining the exonerees' experiences step-by-step. By doing so, this book brings to life the tragedy that is a wrongful conviction and exoneration. While not every exoneree has had similar experiences, the chapters here illustrate the most common themes, from the shock of arrest through a nightmarish trial, from the horrors of imprisonment to the struggles following release.

The first piece, "The Knock on the Door," features a California law student named Gloria Killian who tells her story to renowned writer S. J. Rozan, who then captures innocence lost in an exquisitely horrifying way. In the second chapter, grandmaster Sara Paretsky, whose own personal and complex history includes witnessing egregious acts, takes on the role of police torture in wrongful convictions. In "The Evidence Closes In," best-selling author Laurie R. King masterfully doles out the slow-growing horror and awareness of Ray Towler, a laid-back defendant who once was so sure of the justice system. The shock of hearing the verdict of *guilty* is hammered into brilliant effect by journalist/novelist Brad Parks. Filmmaker-writer Michael Harvey recounts Ken

Wyniemko's initial horrific prison experience, entering a dungeon filled with killers yelling, "Fresh meat, fresh fish!" Thrillermaster Lee Child with Kirk Bloodsworth, a Reacher-esque, real-life hero, in "The Fortune Cookie," describes how Bloodsworth's innocence protected him during his tormented and surreal years in prison. Audrey Edmunds tells, through the husband-and-wife team of John Sheldon (a former prosecutor, defense attorney and judge) and Gayle Lynds (internationally known thriller writer), what it's like to have lived a nightmare of eleven years, away from her babies and her husband. Alton Logan's tale of the specter of Richard Speck is recounted by the celebrated mystery writer Jan Burke. Renowned playwright Arthur Miller's previously unpublished essay on exoneree Peter Reilly, "Luck and the Death Penalty," demonstrates that community outrage can be an important factor in securing exoneration. Sarah Weinman, long known as a critic and nonfiction writer, spins a compelling story of Ginny Lefever's endurance. Legal thriller writer (and criminal defense attorney) Phillip M. Margolin works with William Dillon to tell how the latter was his own lawyer to good effect. Jeff Deskovic's saga of waiting for exoneration is told to Gary Phillips. Mystery writer Jamie Freveletti reveals how Antione Day survived his long incarceration. John Mankiewicz, head writer for the hit television show *House of Cards* and a longtime innocence activist, works with Jerry Miller to depict his surprising exoneration day. Juan Rivera's

FOREWORD

uplifting tale of exoneration and daily resurrection is told
by Laura Caldwell.

This book is not intended as an indictment of the
U.S. legal system nor of the thousands of law enforcement officials, prosecutors, defense attorneys, investigators, judges or juries who make up that system. Nor
does this book claim that the great majority of convicted
persons are innocent of crimes.[6] Rather, the stories
told here acknowledge that as with all human endeavors, the operators of the machinery of justice have flaws
and weaknesses. Police and prosecutors make mistakes,
focusing on the wrong person out of a sincere desire to
protect society. Evidence is mishandled or misinterpreted
by experts. Defense attorneys fail to provide effective
counsel because of overstretched resources or inadequate
training. Juries are swayed by emotions, stoked by the
horrific nature of the crimes or the atmosphere of panic

6   A 2011 Princeton University study ("Growth in the U.S.
     Ex-Felon and Ex-Prisoner Population, 1948–2010") by Sarah
     Shannon, Christopher Uggen, Melissa Thompson, Jason
     Schnittker and Michael Massoglia, based on U.S. Department
     of Justice statistics, estimates that in 2010, 2.5 million per-
     sons were incarcerated in the United States, and another 5.2
     million persons in the population were formerly incarcerated.
     Another source estimates as many as 20 million persons in
     the United States have been convicted of a felony. According
     to the 2015 report of the National Registry of Exonerations,
     ibid., 149 exonerations occurred in 2015, of which 27 involved
     false confessions, 65 included official misconduct and 75 were
     cases in which no crime was actually committed.

and fear. In short, honest members of the community make errors for understandable, even justifiable reasons. Nonetheless, untangling the mistakes can be elusive and very complicated.

Sometimes heartbreaking and harrowing, sometimes comical and endearing, we think *Anatomy of Innocence* will fill your hearts with the stories of these courageous men and women. We are proud of each and every exoneree whose tale is told here, proud that notwithstanding the burdens society placed on them, they never lost hope and persevered. We hope that you come away from this book with a deeper understanding of the price of our flawed justice system.

LAURA CALDWELL
LESLIE S. KLINGER
2016

ANATOMY OF
INNOCENCE

Gloria Killian. © Sameer Abdel-Khalek

1.

THE KNOCK ON THE DOOR

THE ARREST

Gloria Killian (California exoneree),
as told to **S. J. Rozan**

———

FOR MOST EXONEREES, *the initial accusation of guilt isn't the most terrifying part. When you are innocent of a crime—regardless of whether you've been accused of anything before—your innocence plays against you in the initial stages. You want to help; you want to set the record straight; you don't think about incriminating yourself, because you know you're not guilty and that someone else is. Some innocents even head to the police station without being asked. For a law student like Gloria Killian, trained to believe in the merits of the American justice system, her arrest was the shocking beginning of a seventeen-year ordeal.*

1

The knock on the door.

Many people fear it. Some of us hear it in our dreams—it's a nightmare; they've come for you. *They.* When we wake, we realize the knock on the door is a symbol, a crystallization of our own dreads and anxieties. We shake it off and go about our business, knowing it's imaginary, knowing there is no "they," knowing we have nothing to worry about.

When Gloria Killian heard the knock on the door, she was wide awake and it was the middle of the day.

Literally, the middle of a gray Sacramento day: The knock came at the noon hour. The tule fog had settled in, that cold mist that blurs outlines and dims distances. Outdoors was a chilly, unattractive place, but inside—the office at Gloria's boyfriend's auto repair shop—was much more inviting. Not the wooden counter or the vinyl tile floor, but the burnt-orange Naugahyde couch.

Gloria and Rick were going to have a nooner.

They had no customers scheduled at midday that day, a rarity they intended to take advantage of. They lowered the blinds and locked the door. They hadn't seen all that much of each other lately—they didn't live together— and they wanted to make up for lost time. Rick zipped down his grease-spotted mechanic's coveralls and Gloria unbuttoned her blouse. They started in, the caresses, the kisses, more loosened clothes.

The knock on the door.

"Ignore it," Rick whispered into her ear, and then kissed her again. "The shop is closed."

"We have to answer it. *You* have to," she said, pulling her jeans up.

The reason they hadn't been seeing much of each other was the same reason Gloria insisted on answering. Rick was on probation for a DUI. His movements were circumscribed—work, and home to the halfway house where he would live until his probation was complete. His parole officer was expected to make unannounced visits to his workplace to confirm that he was there. Gloria wasn't a lawyer yet, only a law student, but she knew it would be bad if they didn't find Rick at work. She didn't want Rick to compound his troubles; she certainly didn't want him inside. Inside, she'd heard, was a bad place to be.

Gloria Killian buttoned her blouse and smoothed her hair while Rick unlocked the office door. Gloria was smiling; why wouldn't she be? Parole officer, customer or door-to-door salesman, whoever it was, they'd be quickly dispensed with, and she and Rick would return to their afternoon delight.

Two tall, grim men stood in the repair shop yard. "Is Gloria Killian here?" one of them said.

"Right here." Gloria walked to the door.

When they saw her the men stepped closer; they loomed over Gloria, who didn't stand a millimeter over five feet zero. Both showed her Sacramento PD badges. "Are you Gloria Killian?"

Well, she was, and so she said so. She and Rick exchanged confused glances. Cops here, but not about Rick's DUI? Gloria turned to the pair and smiled again, though she wished they'd each take a step back, these large men. They didn't return her smile. "Do you know Virgil Fletcher?"

"Oh." She said it out loud.

This might take longer than *Sorry, good-bye, Rick and I are busy.*

Virgil Fletcher was Gloria's roommate.

A few months earlier Gloria's apartment had been broken into, everything but her clothes taken. She became afraid to stay there. A law student, she worked only part-time, and the need to replace all her possessions, from the alarm clock to the TV and everything in between, was overwhelming. Rick knew a man, Virgil Fletcher, a big old white-bearded Santa Claus of a guy, courtly and very neat. Virgil needed someone to clean his house and cook, and was offering a room and a small salary if he found a person who'd do those things for him. Gloria didn't mind cleaning, loved cooking and was comforted by the idea of not living alone for a time. A deal was struck.

Virgil had co-owned a coin shop in Sacramento. By the time Gloria moved into his house, he'd sold his interest in it, but he'd been in the business long enough that he knew most of the collectors in the Sacramento area.

Gloria and Virgil were watching TV together, a few days before the knock on the office door, when the news reported that a Sacramento coin collector named Ed Davies and his wife, Grace, had been robbed and shot in a home invasion. The solemn-faced anchor looked into the camera and said that the collector had lived but his wife had died.

"Oh my God," Gloria said.

"Oh my God is right. I know those people," Virgil said.

The police questioned Virgil for information about the break-in, the murder. Gloria imagined they were questioning a good number of people in the Sacramento coin-collecting community. It was a community she didn't know well; she'd been to Virgil's shop but she'd never worked there, and she had no interest in coins. One thing she did know, though, was that teddy-bear Virgil couldn't have had anything to do with this crime. A man who was bothered when the cat threw up on the floor? Could he beat and shoot and rob people he knew? No possible way.

Cops are the same everywhere, Gloria thought, *they get an idea about who's guilty, and it's as though they strap on blinders.* "Of course I know Virgil," she said. "I just talked to him last night."

"Can you come down to the Sacramento Detective Bureau and answer a few questions?"

She sighed for the pleasant afternoon she and Rick now wouldn't have.

"Sure," she said. Because the sooner the cops got the idea of Virgil's involvement out of their heads, the sooner they could start looking for the actual murderers.

The grim men didn't thank her. They didn't smile. They stood dourly waiting as she gathered up her purse, her long sweater-coat. Rick, who'd been standing silently by the door, squeezed her hand as she went out.

Now, Gloria was a kidder, a teaser. She didn't know why these men were so sour but she thought she'd joke with them a little. It was clear to her what she and Rick had been doing when interrupted, so obvious that she was straightening her quickly buttoned blouse when Rick opened the door, that she thought these men must have noticed it too. What the hell, might as well start there.

"You guys have terrible timing, you know," she said as she left the shop. "I always get caught."

No smile. No reaction. They flanked her, one on each side, and as they headed for the sidewalk another man— where had he come from?—fell in behind. *Weird*, Gloria thought. The two-man team put her in the back of an unmarked blue Crown Vic. The third man drove off on his own. He was only there to join the escort? Was this SOP for taking someone in for questioning?

The streets of downtown Sacramento are lined with two types of buildings. Stately Victorian homes rub elbows with public buildings from the same grand era, and also with undistinguished modern office blocks, not beautiful but not ugly enough to be interesting. As the car rolled down the street, Gloria, in the rear seat, began to fidget. The feeling she'd had—that this was weird—continued to grow.

"Can I have a cigarette?" Gloria asked.

"No problem," said one of the cops.

"I don't see an ashtray." Gloria slipped a Marlboro Light out of the pack they handed her.

"Just roll down the window."

"Oh, okay." She flicked her lighter. "Didn't want you to think I was planning to jump out."

Again, no smile, nothing. Damn, what did they teach these guys in cop school?

In front of a buff-colored three-story building, one of the dull-as-dishwater modern ones, the cop who was driving parked the car and both cops got out. They took Gloria out, too, and into the lobby. Up in an elevator to the second floor. Turned out this boring building was roof-to-basement law enforcement. Who knew?

The second floor was given over to the Sheriff's Detective Bureau. The tall cops took Gloria to a small room with a table and four wooden chairs.

"Someone will be right with you," one of them said, and they left.

The second one out locked the door behind him.

Gloria heard the lock click and thought, *weirder and weirder.* Did witnesses who came in voluntarily bolt out of here so often that you had to lock them in? She looked around. The room held nothing at all. No trash basket, no posters about being a blood donor. No mirrored walls where cops could watch from the other side. It was neither cold nor hot. Fluorescent lights, scuffed vinyl floor. She sat on a wooden chair and waited.

Twenty-five minutes later Gloria was still waiting. It didn't take her legal training to understand what this was. It's an old cop trick: Let the suspects stew, let them fidget, let them worry. Breaks them down more easily when the interrogation starts.

Except she wasn't a suspect, she was a witness. Or not even. She hadn't *witnessed* anything. Did they think she was so close to Virgil that she'd lie for him? That she needed to be softened up before she'd tell the truth about Virgil's involvement in the Davies robbery, in Grace Davies's murder?

Well, the truth was, there was no way Virgil could have done it. And if by any strange chance Gloria was wrong about that and he was involved, she knew nothing at all about it and had nothing to offer.

It was close to half an hour since she'd been put in the room when the door opened and two new cops came in.

"Can we please get this started?" she said.

They said they were sheriff's investigators. Neither was particularly big or particularly intimidating, in sport jackets and slacks. One was Machen, the other was Reid. One sat beside her, the other across the table. One stayed silent. The other started reading something to her.

"Miranda rights," she said, alarmed.

"Yeah," said Reid. "Though you probably already know them."

That statement was neither complimentary, nor matter-of-fact. It was said with a covert sneer. *You're a law student,* Gloria read on Reid's face, *you think you're so smart.*

After the Miranda rights Reid asked her if she wanted an attorney, as the Miranda warning required him to do.

"Why would I want an attorney?"

She knew nothing about the robbery, the murder or Virgil's involvement in them. If she asked for a lawyer, she'd be stuck here for however long it took for one to arrive. She had nothing to say that could get her in trouble, nothing for an attorney to advise her to keep quiet about, and she'd already been here more than long enough.

"No," Gloria said.

"You waive your right to an attorney?"

"Yes, sure. I do."

"Good," said Reid. "That'll make this go faster. We know you were involved in the Davies murder, Gloria. Tell us about it."

What?

Maybe she'd heard wrong. So she asked, "What did you say?"

"We know you were involved. In fact, you planned it. You were the mastermind. Tell us about it."

"You're wrong. You're completely wrong. What are you talking about?"

"You planned it. We know about that. When did you first get the idea? Where did you meet Ed Davies, at Virgil's shop? Or somewhere else?"

"I don't know what you're talking about. I've never met him."

"You planned this crime, Gloria. It'd be better if you told us about it now."

"No, I didn't. I don't know anything about it."

"You planned it."

"I didn't."

"We know you were involved."

"I wasn't!"

This surreal dialogue went on for two hours. Nothing was accomplished. Neither side budged. Gloria, because she was telling the truth. She hadn't masterminded this crime, had had nothing to do with it. The first she'd heard of it was on TV. The cops, although they presented Gloria with nothing, no hint of why they were so sure she was involved, kept going, kept saying the same things over and over.

"We know you were involved. We know. Tell us."

Then Reid, who'd done most of the talking, looked at his watch and stood up. "Gloria Killian, you're under arrest for the murder of Grace Davies."

"What? Wait, *what?*"

"Please stand up and put your hands behind your back."

Dazed, stunned, disoriented, Gloria stood. They clicked steel cuffs onto her wrists and led her out the door, down the hall. Into the elevator, down another hall, to a side door.

Reid suddenly shifted gears, became solicitous, concerned.

"There might be a reporter or two out there. They hang around the building, you know. Maybe you want to hide your face?"

I'm being arrested. What? Hide. I don't understand. Why hide? Arrested. What?

Gloria was too bewildered to respond. Reid pulled her long sweater-coat up over her head. With one hand clamped onto her arm, he opened the door to the building's side lot.

Flashbulbs exploded. Voices yelled, "Gloria! Gloria! Over here! Anything to say? Gloria!"

And there she was, Gloria Killian, sweater-coat over her head, making her way to a police car to ride to the jail to get booked.

That was why the circular interrogation, unproductive but long.

That was why the glance at the watch and the interview's sudden end.

That was why Reid's unexpected solicitude.

They'd arrested a suspect in the Davies murder, alerted the reporters and perp-walked Gloria Killian right onto the five o'clock news.

...

Gloria Killian was released after four-and-a-half months in county jail for lack of evidence. Instead, a mutual friend of hers and Davies's, Gary Masse, was convicted of Davies's murder and sentenced to life without the possibility of parole. When Masse was jailed, he offered to testify against Gloria, alleging that she was the "mastermind" behind the killing. On the basis of his testimony, Gloria was rearrested and tried, convicted and sentenced to thirty-two years to life for the murder of Davies. After ten years of imprisonment, a new investigation uncovered evidence that Masse's testimony against Gloria was "purchased" in exchange for a substantial reduction in his sentence. The agreement had never been disclosed to the defense. Gloria served almost seventeen years before the 9th Circuit Court of Appeals overturned her conviction. Since her release, Gloria has raised money to help women prisoners. She founded an advocacy group, the Action Committee for Women in Prison, and she has also written a book titled Full Circle.

S. J. ROZAN is an award-winning writer of detective fiction and thrillers. She writes a series about Lydia Chin and Bill Smith, often with a significant Chinese element, and also cowrites a paranormal thriller series under the pseudonym "Sam Cabot." She is a writing instructor, former architect and lifelong New Yorker.

Editors' Note

The National Registry of Exonerations tabulates information regarding persons who were wrongfully convicted and ultimately exonerated, beginning with exonerations that took place after 1988. As of October 2016, the Registry listed 1,900 exonerations; 90 percent of the exonerees were identified as male; 10 percent identified as female; 46 percent were black; 40 percent white; 12 percent Hispanic; and 2 percent classed as Native American, Asian or other races. Almost 10 percent of the exonerees in the Registry were under age eighteen on the date of the reported crime; nearly half were twenty-five years old or less.

David Bates, left, with exoneree Michael Evans, Life After Innocence director Laura Caldwell and LAI adjunct professor Meghan Fahey Monty

2.

THE TRIP TO DOTY ROAD

THE INTERROGATION

David Bates (Illinois exoneree), *as told to* Sara Paretsky

FEW CAN IMAGINE *any circumstances that would lead them to confess to a crime they didn't commit, especially if the crime is a heinous one. But false confessions happen often, sometimes because the people who confess are overwhelmed and bewildered: They are alone, and interrogators are trained to keep suspects off balance. Under current legal rules, there are few restrictions on the lies that interrogators can tell the subject, so all the following are entirely permissible—"Your companion confessed," "We have physical evidence linking you to the scene" and often "If you just say this, you can go home." The ultimate tool to obtaining a confession is, far too often, torture—even in the twenty-first century, even in the United States, the bastion of liberty.*

Torture—physical or psychological—changes everything for the victim. Even the spaces between moments of torture become unbearable, as David Bates recounts. His story is one of cruelty that is, sadly, far from unusual: Although the application of physical abuse in interrogations has declined sharply in the United States and elsewhere, psychological torture, in many forms, is still condoned and takes place every hour of the day in every country in the world and is among the leading causes of wrongful convictions.

Life along Doty Road on Chicago's far South Side takes place in many layers. Heading west from 103rd Street, Doty skirts the city of Chicago's massive graveyard of towed and impounded cars and trucks. Doty then curves south, following the shoreline of Lake Calumet, and passes through the last of the marshes that used to make up the whole shoreline of the land where Chicago was built. Waterbirds of all kinds swim here, people fish— even if it's illegal, the ten-foot-high marsh grasses provide good cover.

Above the marshes stands a mighty hill, covered in grass and wildflowers. They cover the CID landfill—the Calumet Industrial District—a century and a half's worth of garbage trucked in from the three million people in the city. In the 1990s, when the landfill topped out, the city built a golf course over the garbage—one so good that people like Bill Clinton have helicoptered in to play there.

In 1983, garbage trucks were still hauling waste there twenty-four hours a day. At the bottom, along with the ducks and herons, stood the old steel mills, which had begun shutting down three years earlier. Today, nothing is left of the mills, although chemical companies are still doing business. Then as now, homeless people with feral dogs live in the swamps, and waste haulers dump loads illegally into the fragile marshes.

Doty Road is a place where no one's screams are heard, where a dead body could lie undiscovered forever in the marshes and chemical wastes. Doty Road: it's where the police threatened to take David Bates if he didn't confess to a murder where they wanted a fast solution.

David Bates had just turned eighteen on October 29, 1983, when a crew of uniforms and detectives came to the back door of his parents' home at 96th and Wentworth. It was about 7:30 in the morning. One held a .357 in Bates's mother's face and demanded to speak to her son.

"Just to ask him some questions," they said, "a routine inquiry, no need for you to go to the police station with him. We'll bring him back," they said. Which they did. Eleven years later.

David was the third child of Lee and Rosa Lee Bates. His father was a Chicago native, but his mother had come to Chicago from Louisiana in the 1950s, part of the second Great Migration, looking for a better life for themselves and their children. David's mother had only a second-grade education, but she and her husband built a successful restaurant and catering business, preparing some of Chicago's best soul food.

David's parents also provided a way station on what David calls a second underground railroad. As African Americans fled lynch mobs, forcible property seizures, rape, murder—and segregation—in the South, the Bates family provided a place to sleep while the new arrivals got on their feet. At Rosa Lee Bates's funeral, the pastor asked how many in the church that day had found a temporary home with Mrs. Bates. Over a hundred people raised their hands.

David didn't know why the police came for him that October morning. He didn't know they had already put him in the frame for the murder of a drug dealer named Leon Barkan, which had happened two days earlier.

"I knew about it—it happened half a mile from my home," David says. "And I won't claim I was a saint. I'd served as a lookout for the Gangster Disciples, mostly looking for excitement, but murder was way outside my experience. And Barkan's murder—that had nothing to do with me or anyone I knew."

Even if David Bates had been a saint, it wouldn't necessarily have protected him from the Area Two detectives: they didn't need any particular rationale to take in an African American for questioning—honor students, nurses, murderers, armed robbers, medical equipment installers—they all received equal treatment at the hands of the law in Area Two.

David was taken to Area Two headquarters on 111th Street, about three miles from his home. He was handcuffed to a wall and left there alone. After two hours, two detectives appeared.

"Tell us about Leon Barkan's murder. We know you were at 92nd and Harvard. Tell us what you did and the state's attorney will go easy on you. What did you do with the gun?"

All the time they were shouting questions at him, they were slapping, kicking and punching him. David couldn't see their badges; he didn't learn their names.

"I memorized their faces and their mannerisms. One had curly hair and glasses, so I called him Curly. The other I thought of as Moustache."

David adds, "I kept saying I didn't know anything. This went on about forty-five minutes and then they left me alone again, still handcuffed to the wall. The funny thing is, what they were doing didn't seem criminal at first, it just seemed part of the territory, of being a black kid on the South Side."

He was left alone, still cuffed to the wall, trying to assess the situation logically. He couldn't understand why Curly and Moustache thought he had murdered Leon Barkan. In his naïveté he thought he could use logic to show them that their suspicions were wrong. Logic and evidence didn't play a role at Area Two, as David learned over the course of the next very long day.

"The second session, that was what put me on alert. They came in and started right away saying, 'We heard this about you, that you were at 92nd and Harvard when Barkan was killed. Someone told us they saw you there, they saw you with a gun.'

"They kept kicking and beating me and calling me names. I thought I could handle it, but when they left, Curly said, 'We've been playing with you. After this, they'll take you apart and you won't be coming back. They'll take you to Doty Road.'"

David had just turned eighteen. He was alone. He had been chained to a ring screwed into the wall for many hours. He knew what "Doty Road" meant. He was terrified.

The ring in the wall was part of an organized setup for committing torture by Area Two detectives. (The Chicago Police Department has twenty-five districts divided now among three areas; in 1983 there were five areas. The area headquarters are where investigative officers for homicide, violent crimes, gangs, narcotics and other major offenses work.)

In 1983, when David Bates was in custody, he knew nothing about the pattern and practice of torture at Area Two. He only knew that he needed to summon whatever mental and physical resources he had to cope with what might come next. In his ignorance, he thought he could be strong enough to stand up to whatever the detectives might do.

After another interval, perhaps two hours, Curly returned with a different detective, not Moustache. They unhooked him from the ring in the wall and put him in a chair with his hands cuffed behind his back. Curly was in front, the other man behind.

"Before I knew it, they put something over my head," David recalls. "I couldn't breathe, there was something around my neck. I can't remember if I passed out, but that's when I knew everything they were doing wasn't right."

They took the bag from his head. To his horror and disgust, David could see that Curly was sexually aroused by the torture he was committing. David felt a deep sense of shame, as though he himself had provoked the arousal. It was well over a decade before David could bear to think—let alone talk about—Curly's sexual excitement. He also felt a deep sense of humiliation because, he says, he reverted to feeling and responding like a small child. "Whatever toughness I thought I had—I became what they wanted me to be—and so they left off."

They left him alone again. The time between this session and the next was the worst time. After the third session, David says, "I wanted to save myself. I decided that when the detectives came back in, I would scream as loudly as possible. I wanted them to be held accountable."

When the men came back in, David hollered at the

top of his voice. "They'd been doing it for so many years, with so many people, they were prepared for any response," David says. "And they punched me in the stomach, they put the bag back over my head, they suffocated me again."

After he'd been in the interrogation room for about twenty-four hours, a fresh set of detectives came in. One officer unchained him and spoke to him sympathetically, saying he'd heard what "those guys"—Curly and Moustache—had been doing. The officer claimed he wanted to help David. He told him what to say, how to phrase a confession of a murder he had not committed, "so you won't have to deal with those guys."

At this point, David had not been allowed to use a bathroom, nor been given anything to eat or drink. The state of his clothes and of his body was deeply shaming to him. Nonetheless, he was so new to police interrogation that he still believed the law would be on his side, if he could only find someone to listen to him.

The officer took David to the office of the assistant state's attorney assigned to that police district. David thought his troubles were over. The law would now save him. He cried out how glad he was to see the state's attorney and started to recount his ordeal. The state's attorney turned to the officer and asked if any torture had taken place.

David said the officer took him out to the hall. "He told me if I didn't sign the confession, he would hand me back to Curly and Moustache. He repeated that they would take me out to Doty Road. No one I knew ever heard of Doty Road like that. We all knew where it was, but we never heard it used as a threat, and this sounded like they were going to kill me if I didn't confess."

And so David went back to the state's attorney's office. The assistant on duty summoned his court reporter. With the officer's help, the assistant state's attorney dictated a confession that David signed; the confession included details of Leon Barkan's murder.

The confession was as humiliating as the torture itself. It destroyed part of David's sense of who he was. He had believed he was a strong person, but he had been humiliated and degraded. His personal code of behavior included not signing confessions, not giving in to coercion, but within two days of his arrest, he had done exactly that.

It's been more than thirty years since David Bates signed that confession, but the effects of torture still linger in his mind and body. He was incarcerated for eleven years for a crime he didn't commit. During that time, he never spoke to anyone of the torture that put him behind bars. No one at Area Two, no one in the courtroom where his trial took place, had listened to him or believed him when he had tried to explain himself. He felt completely alone and isolated in his humiliation. He kept it to himself for fear that his fellow inmates might view him as somehow lacking in courage.

He learned later that a friend of his, Gregory Banks, had been tortured into naming David the day before his own arrest. He learned that the bag that had been used to suffocate him was the vinyl cover to an IBM typewriter. He also learned that many of the men he was incarcerated with carried the same shaming secret he did.

Thirty-plus years after his torture, twenty years after his exoneration, David Bates has days where he can't walk. The powerlessness he felt at his torturers' hands sweeps through his body, paralyzing him. Many nights he wakes up drenched with sweat, his feet throbbing in pain.

Torture recurs in the minds and bodies of survivors because the very effect of torture is to make people feel that they were complicit in what happened to them. Their bodies betrayed them and so they feel a sense of betrayal clear through the core of their being.

When David turned to the assistant state's attorney and was then betrayed by him, it further rattled his sense of reality. The threat of being sent to Doty Road—"you'll never come back"—was in effect a death threat against David Bates. Small wonder his body continues to throw out symptoms of paralysis.

About twenty detectives took part in torturing people in custody over a period of perhaps nineteen years. Torture included using an electric cattle prod on people's genitals and bare skin—often in the back of a squad car;

attaching electrodes to the ears and to the genitals and running electric currents through them; suffocating people in custody; waterboarding; suspending people by their arms with their feet off the floor; and depriving people of sleep, food, water and toilets.

Because Chicago has permitted only limited investigation into the officers involved, and for many years resisted any investigation into the many reports of torture, it's impossible to know when the practice began. Dr. Robert Kirschner, former deputy chief medical examiner for Cook County, first realized he was seeing clear signs of torture on a man in custody in 1982. He and others began raising the issue with the Cook County state's attorney, but got no response.

For many people undergoing torture, a certain dementia sets in: We are brought up to believe that the police and the courts, however flawed, represent justice. When the people we expect to rescue us fail us, when they turn out to be participants in the torture, it creates a shocking and irrecoverable sense of abandonment, of a world turned upside down. People around the world who work with survivors of torture say it is impossible to know how long the aftershocks linger—they can recur decades after the survivor has resumed an ordinary life.

David Bates is a survivor but is understandably angry. The detectives took not just eleven years of his life, but his sense of self. The city paid him a small

sum when he was exonerated, while it has spent millions
defending the cops who tortured him.

———

SARA PARETSKY has been a crusader all her life.
Most of her crusading has taken the form of fiction, her
incandescent series of seventeen novels about female pri-
vate investigator V. I. Warshawski. Sara was a founder of
Sisters in Crime, the preeminent organization for women
crime writers, and served in 2015 as the president of the
Mystery Writers of America. She was named a Grand
Master, a lifetime achievement award, by the Mystery
Writers of America in 2011.

Editors' Note

Almost 13 percent of the cases recorded in the National
Registry of Exonerations included false confessions as at
least part of the basis of conviction. The Innocence Project
estimates that as many as 25 percent of the DNA exonerations included coerced false confessions or incriminating
statements. (DNA makes up for less than a fourth of all
cases overturned following wrongful conviction.) Such
coercion may involve physical torture, psychological torture and threats of harsher treatment if the interrogated
person fails to "cooperate," followed by promises that the
interrogee can go home.

Ray Towler

3.

THE EVIDENCE CLOSES IN

THE TRIAL

Ray Towler (Ohio exoneree), *as told to*
Laurie R. King

———

*EVERYONE HAS SEEN trials—on television, in
film, reading about them in books. Everyone knows that
trials are where the truth is discovered and justice is dispensed, where an impartial judge or jury sifts through the
evidence and the arguments of prosecutors and defense
attorneys, and arrives at a just result. But what if that
doesn't happen? What if the trial resembles an event out
of Kafka, where fantasy is endorsed as reality, and the
truth is left knocking at the door?*

Day One: Friday
This courtroom is the whitest place Ray Towler has been
for a long time. The man beside him is white, like the

man at the other table. The judge is an old white man in a black robe, and the black faces that passed through the jury box were one by one pushed out in yesterday's selection, leaving white, white, white.

The blackest things here are his family behind him, and Raymond Towler, black man on trial for . . . for something he didn't even want to think about.

That poor little thing. Jennifer was her name. Eleven years old. They'd made her come in on Wednesday, so the two lawyers could fight over who got to use what evidence, and Ray got his first look at this tiny creature who he'd been accused of, of . . .

She was a *baby*. Sure, some sixth-graders were halfway to women, but not Jennie. She didn't look any older than Ray's ten-year-old kid sister, Angie—or his niece Michelle, who was nine. When the judge talked to her about telling the truth two days ago, he'd used the example of Pinocchio's nose growing, that's how much of a baby she was.

And when she stuck out her little baby's finger and pointed it at him, well, it made him feel sick. Really sick. Poor little thing, she'd probably never seen a black man up close until . . . until what happened to her in the park last May. And with Ray sitting where Bad Men sit, well. He just hoped she didn't feel too bad about things later, when this was cleared up. It wasn't her fault.

Today was the first day of the trial itself and the third day he'd come here. That first time had been the preliminary hearing—a sort of minitrial, when Jennie and her boy cousin, along with the two grown-up witnesses and the park cop, had sat and told the judge how absolutely sure they were that Raymond Towler was the man they'd seen in the park that day with the two kids.

Prosecutor: *The black male sitting at the table?*

Witness: *Yes.*

Prosecutor: *Your Honor, may the record indicate that the witness identified the defendant, Raymond Towler?*

Judge: *The record may so indicate.*

One after another, those fingers pointed. So his lawyer, Gold—a hard-of-hearing old guy with shaky hands and white socks (*Who wears white socks with shoes like that?*)—lost his motion to have their eyewitness testimony left out. Then yesterday jurors came in and were excused, leaving what his mom would call a baker's dozen, and Ray tried not to think of thirteen as bad luck. This morning they'd all gone on a field trip to see where . . . that thing happened, but now they were back and here they were, settling down to the lawyers' opening statements.

The prosecutor went first. The man reminded Ray of a drill sergeant he'd had in Fort Dix, hard and loud. He was telling the jury every little detail of what had happened and what he was going to show them in order to prove Ray did it—no surprises here, not like a *Quincy, M.E.* or *Columbo* show. Ray knew he ought to be paying attention but it was tough, with his mind jumping all over the place like this, thinking about that little baby girl and those people who said he'd done this. Crazy, wasn't it? Him, Ray Towler? Laid-back, easygoing Ray? Ray was about the last person in Cleveland who'd do something awful to a couple of kids. All Ray wanted to do was play his music and smoke a doobie now and then.

Might be nice to have a real job, but in Cleveland? Nothing here for a twenty-four-year-old with an Army GED and some music and art skills. Maybe he should reenlist. Or take a training course somewhere. Once this was out of the way. Not that a young black man had much chance for a future, here. Black men were expected to be angry and up to no good. Who'd expect a young man with dark skin and a big beard to be easygoing? But that was him. Polite and patient, that was the best way to get along. Trust the system. Things would work out.

It looked like the prosecutor was about finished. Nearly twenty minutes, he'd been going on about things Ray really didn't want to think about. Now it was time for Gold to talk, to tell those thirteen people how it was all a mistake, that he was sorry but really, these so-called witnesses were just dead wrong. Ray settled in to listen.

Thank you, your Honor, Mr. Levi and ladies and gentlemen of the jury, good afternoon. It's still morning—good morning, ladies and gentlemen of the jury. As the evidence in this case develops, you will be convinced that the defendant is innocent, and when you go back to your deliberating room, you will bring back a verdict of not guilty. Thank you very much.

Wait—what? That was *it*, the guy was finished? The judge was saying it was time for lunch?

They took Ray out. He didn't have much of an appetite.

After lunch the kid—the little girl's twelve-year-old cousin, Tim, who now had a cast on his arm—told the jury the same things he'd said to the judge on Wednesday, although he'd had time to smooth out the details since then. With someone's help, maybe? Or was "Me and Jennie looked at each other mysteriously, shockingly, and then he pulled out a gun" how kids talked these days? Sounded like TV, for sure. That black male in the park (the only black male in the park that day, everyone agreed) had told the kids there was a hurt deer back among the trees and would they come see. Then once away from the bike path, he'd pulled the gun on them, forced them to lie down, and . . .

Honestly, did anything about that sound like Ray Towler? A deer in the woods? In Cleveland? Who was he, Daniel Boone or something? And that description, the same from them all: sunglasses and stubble. Ray's beard had been growing since he got out of the Army five years ago. And even the kid admitted it was so dark back in the woods he couldn't see what was going on.

But when Gold started his cross-examination, the prosecutor kept interrupting, and Gold got irritated and they and the judge started to squabble, which was kind of embarrassing. Though he did get Tim to admit that what he'd seen was mostly the black man's back, when he and Jennie followed the guy to see the deer.

The next witness was one of the grown-ups, the man, who said the same: black male, sunglasses, the beginnings of a beard. He didn't remember anything about how the man looked other than "black." And he'd only told the park police about it after they'd ticketed him for public drinking and shown him that flier with the sketch made from Timmy's description. Which looked nothing like Ray Towler, as far as Ray could see. No, *of course* the guy hadn't been drinking the day he'd seen this black male.

Your Honor, may the record indicate that the witness identified the defendant, Raymond Towler?

The record may so indicate.

Day Two: Monday

It wasn't a very good weekend, and today was going to be rough. But once today was over, they could begin to put Ray's side of things in front of the jury.

Little Jennie took the stand.

She looked even smaller than she had on Wednesday, and her voice went so quiet that Gold kept asking the judge to make her speak up. The prosecutor took her through the story—bicycles, picnic, deer, black man—

34

and when he had her point him out, the black man at the table, Ray felt his family wince behind him. The details the prosecutor made her give were things no little girl should have to talk about in public—the straps of her jumper, the underwear in the evidence envelope. Then things got ugly.

Ray didn't catch it at first. All along, the prosecutor had been asking the witnesses about "this man" being here and "this man" doing that, meaning the guy in the park. But somehow, "this man" changed to "the defendant." The first time it happened and Gold shot up to object, Ray wasn't quite sure why. The judge over-ruled it. Then Gold insisted on going up to talk to the judge (without the jury hearing—they called this a side-bar) and afterward, the judge said okay, and asked the prosecutor to rephrase the question. But the prosecutor then used the same phrase: "Did the defendant leave?" Gold objected; the judge suggested again that counsel rephrase it. This happened not just once, but over and over, like a hammer driving a nail, until the prosecutor stood up in front of the jury and asked that little girl: "What did this defendant do after he had inserted his penis into your vagina?"

Ray felt like he'd been hit in the gut. Gold started to shout—out loud, at the judge, in the hearing range of the jury, demanding a mistrial.

Because "the defendant" wasn't some black man in a park; "the defendant" meant Raymond Towler, sitting right there with that little girl saying in front of God and everyone that he'd done unspeakable, obscene things to her.

Of course, there would be no mistrial. After that last time, the prosecutor used "this individual." But everyone in the courtroom heard "Ray Towler," and everyone in the jury box had the idea of a black man's penis and a little girl's private parts locked in their brains.

Three short questions later, the prosecutor sealed it by having little Jennie point her finger at him.

Let the record reflect that the witness identified the defendant, Raymond Towler.

The rest of her testimony hardly mattered. Did any juror even notice that she'd never told the police her attacker had a beard? Who cared anymore that she'd been with her cousin and the two grown-up witnesses when she looked at the pictures, perhaps subtly pressured to confirm the identification? Even Ray only noticed afterward that she'd kept saying "the black guy" rather than "he," meaning Ray.

After lunch, when Gold was trying to question her, the prosecutor kept interrupting, sniping at him, throwing up objections. Ray was so glad when they finally let the poor child go—until the emergency room doctor sat down. Between the man's heavy Indian accent and his scientific terms, the only thing anyone heard were words like "semen" and "laceration."

He was as glad as everyone else when the seat was taken over by the ranger who'd been on duty that day, who had put the two kids in the back of his cruiser to drive them around looking for the black male, then taken them to the hospital where the strange hands of the Indian doctor waited for the girl.

As court was dismissed for the day, a thought occurred to Ray: *Back on that day in May, when had anyone thought to give that poor terrified child a hug?*

Day Three: Tuesday

Today the prosecutor had a stack of witnesses, mostly park policemen. Now, Ray never had any particular problems with the police. Yes, to be young and black in Cleveland was to be hassled, but he'd been raised to believe that the police do the right thing, eventually, and he'd lived long enough to know how it worked: They picked you up, they pushed you around a little and they let you go. Part of the game. It was what he'd expected, back in June when they arrested him.

Anyway, he had no particular beef with the cops, in spite of everything. The first one was explaining about the traffic detail that had actually snagged Ray, two weeks after the rape, for a "rolling stop" as he went through the park. Which he was positive he hadn't in fact done—the park was the kind of place a black man watched himself, so he always took care to stop, to signal, to be polite there, *always*.

Then when the police had asked Ray to come in to have his picture taken after that traffic stop, he'd been all, "No problem, happy to come along." Ray knew *he* hadn't done any robberies, which they said they'd had in the area. Just act polite, don't give them any excuse to come down on you, and they'd lose interest. In fact, he'd expected it to end pretty much right away, after they put him in their cruiser and drove him around to where some little girl stood (Was it this kid Jennie? He wished he could remember more clearly) and they asked her if this was the guy. She looked through the window at him and said no, at which point Ray settled back, knowing it was just one of those things, on its way to being cleared up.

He didn't know that the photo they took would end up getting shown to the kids and the grown-ups. He couldn't know that they would all four decide that Raymond Towler, a stocky guy with a big beard, was the thin black man with the stubble and sunglasses who'd been walking along the bike path that Sunday afternoon. Ray couldn't know that he'd end up here, listening to the girl testify about whizzing around on skates and seeing the man three times (once from behind—and for a total of less than a minute). He couldn't have known that no one would doubt her identifying him, even though at the time, she'd only noted a man wearing street clothes rather than shorts, and didn't remember any beard—yet when she'd been shown the photos three weeks later, she picked Ray out, as she picked him out across the courtroom now.

Then came the expert witness, a criminologist who could magically tell through his microscope that two curly black hairs were not only Negro, and pubic, but that they appeared identical to the sample Raymond had volunteered to the police.

The criminologist's testimony was interrupted by a lot of objections, and Gold tried to get it dismissed as a "possibility" rather than a "probability," but that didn't happen, either.

At least that marked the end of the prosecutor's case. Tomorrow Ray would present his side of things—and of course he would testify, he had nothing to hide. Nothing to be ashamed of beyond sleeping in on the day of the crime and not having a regular job. Tomorrow was when it would all be sorted out, and he'd shake hands with Gold and go home to another party with the family and be left hoping that little girl and her cousin didn't feel too much of a guilty burden about what they'd put him through.

Except . . . the judge called him and Gold into his office. To talk about a plea. And then the judge sent Gold out of the room. He looked at Ray and pointed at the view out his high-up window at the lake and the boats and the world spreading out beyond, gorgeous and glittering.

"If you don't take the deal," the judge told him, "you'll never see that lake again."

A *deal*? Somebody in jail that summer had said he should plead out, and he'd be free in two years. And even though the guy hadn't seemed on the up-and-up, like maybe he was working for the cops, here was the judge himself telling Ray that same thing. Maybe he should sign. Maybe that would make everything go away. But that would mean admitting to something he hadn't done—something twisted and horrible and disgusting. It meant he'd have to stand there and confess to this . . . thing some man had done, knowing his family was hearing—knowing little Angie and Michelle would never look at him the same. And without even being really sure how much prison time they were talking about.

If the man had given him a firm offer—if he'd even done it with Gold there and approving—Ray might have been tempted by all that glittering promise outside the window. But dazed as he was, and laid back as he might be, a voice inside him said: *Don't sign it. The system will work, eventually.*

So he thanked the judge—no shouting from him, no sir—and turned him down, going back to his cell and his thoughts.

There wasn't much left of the confidence he'd felt a week before. Ray was beginning to feel that until the judge made that offer, his alarm system had been on mute. Not now. Now it was yammering away at the back of his head, making the cell very cold and dark indeed.

Day Four: Wednesday
Which brought them to the defense.

Gold had explained to Ray that he didn't have to testify on his own defense, but Ray knew there was no way he could sit there in court, his family listening to the things these people had been saying about the defendant, without speaking up. The charges were ridiculous and hurtful, but they'd also started to scare him. At first he'd thought, *How can they even think of putting this on me?* Now it was more like, *How can I stop them?*

And so he got up and moved into the box where his string of accusers had sat, and he took the oath and he let Gold coax the story out of him. He wanted to trust the jurors—a week ago, he *had* trusted them—to see how crazy this terrible accusation was. Wanted them to see that here was one black man who was just a guy, a young man who'd served his country, who loved his mother, who swept the garage so his sister and niece could roller skate around when it was raining. A guy who respected the world even if it wouldn't give him a job. A person who never hurt any little girl in his life. Who had been home with his family all day, miles away from where little Jennie had been attacked.

But when Gold sat down and the prosecutor got up, all his details seemed to fall to pieces. Ray couldn't remember what TV channel they'd been watching, or what time he'd gone to bed. And really, hadn't he left the Army just an inch from a dishonorable discharge? On and on, getting Ray so confused he began to wonder if maybe he really was just a shiftless no-good living off his mother, in a house that was maybe only five minutes from the park, who was probably lying about his beard and his car registration and everything else. At the end of it, Ray wouldn't have been too surprised to have the man suggest that his sister and niece weren't safe, living in the same house as him.

His mom came then, solid and sure. Just seeing her helped, though really, whose mother wouldn't take her son's side? Then Gold brought in the girls, first little Angie and then Ray's sister, Michelle. Good girls, and he'd have given a lot to save them from having to come to this room full of white faces asking a load of idiotic questions.

Then his brother, and sure enough, that little matter of an armed robbery came out. Oops. Then Ray's cousin, and then a friend—a friend whose assurance that Ray was a good guy got so broken up by objections and back tracking, even Ray himself couldn't follow what was being said. One last character witness: an old, loyal friend of his mom's, who raised her head and said proudly that she'd known Raymond Towler since his birth and he'd always been a speaker of the truth. But when she was turned over to the prosecutor, the man made her admit that maybe she didn't know Ray as well as she thought, and when he asked her for a specific example of when he'd told the truth about a matter, naturally she couldn't come up with one.

Day Five: Thursday
Ray sat in his chair and listened to the two lawyers slam away at each other like bristling dogs, Gold trying to

get all kinds of evidence put aside, the prosecutor and judge having nothing to do with it. It was cold in the courtroom. Or maybe it was just Ray. He felt dazed, and empty, and scared.

Finally, the three men ran out of steam, and the jury was let back in.

Gold had meant to call another witness, the day before, but this morning he just rested his case. The prosecutor dragged the park lieutenant back in front of the jury, with another round of discussion about the beard, and then it was time for closing arguments.

The prosecutor went first, an unbroken twenty-minute reminder of everything he'd promised to give them during his opening on Friday. He stood in front of the jury, the very model of honesty, and reminded them time and again that they were there because of a little girl "raped by a black man."

As if they could ever forget. As for the beard, it was dismissed with, "Who knows what the state of his beard was?"

Then the prosecutor sat down, and Gold got up.

He waffled around a bit, and just when he was hitting his stride, the prosecutor stepped in with an objection. Four of them, one after another. But even when Gold was permitted a free run, he wasn't exactly passionate about Ray Towler. "He couldn't have been too bad a guy. His brother left him to watch the children, and nothing happened."

That alarm system was sounding so loud in Ray's head, it was hard to hear his lawyer's voice.

When Gold was finished, he told the jury, "You will agree that the prosecutor has not under any conditions proven a crime, an alleged crime, that a crime was committed by the defendant—have proven it beyond a reasonable doubt, to each and every single element as the court will tell you."

Gold himself looked confused when he sat down.

But not the prosecutor. He didn't have to worry anymore about Gold, who'd had his chance, so he brought out his big guns: insinuations about lies, crowing over gaps in the defense, making Ray look like an absolute criminal. There was even a reminder about his brother, "the armed robber with a gun"—and who was to say he hadn't given that gun to Ray? Insults and insinuations, against his mother, her friend and everyone on Ray's side short of his sister and niece.

Ray found it hard to breathe when the man finished. He couldn't bear to look at the jury. *I didn't do anything. I wasn't there. I would never—ever!—touch a little girl that way.*

They had to see that. *Had* to. But he just kept hearing that exchange from the trial:

Do you mean the black male sitting at the table?

Yes.

Your Honor, may the record indicate that the witness identified the defendant, Raymond Towler?

The record may so indicate.

THE JURY DELIBERATED for one morning in the case of Raymond Towler v. State of Ohio. *He was convicted of raping "Jennifer" and sentenced to life plus twelve to forty years. Ray Towler's trial took place in 1981, long before DNA testing was admissible in Ohio courts. More than twenty years after his conviction, Ohio passed a law allowing DNA testing in very limited circumstances. The Ohio Innocence Project immediately teamed with Ray to help him file an application for DNA testing as soon as the law was enacted. As a result of DNA testing, Ray was released. The presiding judge apologized for the miscarriage of justice and fought back tears as she offered him a traditional Irish blessing: "May the road rise to meet you; may the wind be always at your back," and finally, "You're free." Days later, Ray was released from prison after twenty-eight years of being locked up. He was fifty-four years old. Ray was awarded compensation from the state of Ohio.*

———

LAURIE R. KING is the author of twenty-five novels and many other works, including fourteen "Mary Russell" stories, the memoirs of a young woman who marries Sherlock Holmes. Laurie won the Edgar® Award for her first novel, *A Grave Talent*, and has been honored widely and frequently for her writing. She may be unique among mystery writers in holding both an honorary doctorate in theology and membership in the Baker Street Irregulars.

Editors' Note

Ray Towler was a victim of several false witness identifications, as well as inadequate legal representation. Almost one-third of the exonerations included in the National Registry involved mistaken witness identifications (many have multiple factors identified as having contributed to the wrongful conviction). According to the Innocence Project, eyewitness misidentification is the greatest contributing factor to wrongful convictions proven by DNA testing, playing a role in more than 70 percent of convictions overturned through DNA testing nationwide.

Eyewitness identifications are given great credibility by juries (and juries convicted 77 percent of the exonerees whose cases are recorded in the National Registry). U.S. Supreme Court Justice William J. Brennan Jr., in his dissent to *Watkins v. Sowders*,[1] stated that witness testimony is evidence that "juries seem most receptive to, and not inclined to discredit." In fact, Brennan wrote, "All the evidence points rather strikingly to the conclusion that there is almost nothing more convincing [to a jury] than a live human being who takes the stand, points a finger at the defendant, and says, 'That's the one!'"

---

1   449 U.S. 341 (1980).

But Justice Brennan also observed, "At least since *United States v. Wade*, 388 U.S. 218 (1967), the Court has recognized the inherently suspect qualities of eyewitness identification evidence, and described the evidence as 'notoriously unreliable.'" In fact, such evidence has long been suspect. In 1908, pioneering psychologist Hugo Münsterberg's *On the Witness Stand* questioned the reliability of eyewitness identification. Yale law professor Edwin Borchard's groundbreaking 1932 book *Convicting the Innocent*, which studied sixty-five wrongful convictions, concluded that eyewitness misidentification was the leading contributing factor of wrongful convictions.

A number of cities and states have taken steps to address the problem, including requiring blind administration of lineups (in which the administrator does not know the identity of the suspect), admonitions to witnesses that a lineup may not include a suspect and routine recording of identification procedures.

Exoneree Michael Evans, center, with former Life After Innocence students Tyler Cox, left, and Jordan Fries. Courtesy of Life After Innocence

4.

JUST ONE

THE VERDICT

Michael Evans (Illinois exoneree), as told to Brad Parks

AFTER THE ORDEAL of arrest, interrogation and for many, the long wait to tell their story, the trial itself seems like the promised land, the light at the end of the long, dark tunnel, when truth and justice will be delivered. But after hearing people talk about them in unrecognizable ways, the penny drops for the accused: For the members of the jury, sometimes the most uninformed entity in the system, the experience can be agonizing. But that system, for better or for worse, is about to make a decision that will change the life of the exoneree forever.

Sitting in a cage at the Cook County Criminal Courthouse, a few rooms away from the twelve strangers weighing his fate, Michael Evans needed just one person.

One person to end the surreal journey that began on a February morning fourteen months earlier, when police yanked him off the street, threw him into the back of a van and lashed him with a metal belt on their way to the precinct.

One person to look past the heinousness of his alleged crime and realize the detectives in Chicago's Area Two had been more zealous to close the case than to find the real perpetrator.

One person to see through the shifting patchwork of fabrications from the lone eyewitness, a woman who first came forward not to the authorities, but to a man offering a $5,000 reward.

One person to realize Michael—a seventeen-year-old kid who sang in the church choir, had a bit of a stutter and went by the nickname "Smiley"—had neither the violent nature to attempt this act, nor access to the car he would have needed to carry it off.

One person to hang the jury and prevent the guilty verdict that Michael knew, in every part of his soul, did not match the truth.

...

The crime was so notorious, Chicago newspapers—the tabloids and the broadsheets alike—referred to it in their headlines with just one word: "Lisa."

On the evening of January 14, 1976, nine-year-old

Lisa Cabassa left her house on South Saginaw Avenue, on Chicago's South Side. She and her eleven-year-old brother, Ricky, were walking a friend home. Halfway there, complaining of a headache, she turned around. She never made it back. The next morning, shortly before 3 a.m., a man came across her body in an alley two miles away. She had been sexually assaulted and strangled.

After a relentless investigation, police produced two witnesses: a woman who said she saw Michael Evans pull Lisa into an alley, and a man who said Michael led him to Lisa's body on the night of the murder.

There were gaping holes in both stories. And Michael had something going for him many defendants did not: a family that believed in his innocence. His older sister, Clare, worked two jobs so her brother could hire a private attorney, Sam Adam, already becoming locally famous as a tenacious criminal defender.

Still, the first time the case went to trial, even Adam didn't want to go in front of a jury. He felt regular citizens would be overcome by the need to punish *someone* for a crime so horrific and would convict whichever defendant the prosecution put in front of them. Especially when that defendant was a young black man.

Adam opted for a bench trial—and still lost. A judge found Michael Evans guilty on all counts. Then came a reprieve. Before sentencing, the judge vacated his conviction when he learned the prosecution had withheld a key piece of evidence: the female eyewitness had received $1,250 from the government to relocate her family, which the judge felt may have motivated her testimony.

During the interlude between the first and second trials, the defense got another huge break. The man who said Michael showed him the body recanted, admitting he concocted the entire story under coercion from the police. Bolstered by that victory, and with the prosecution's case looking weaker than ever, Adam decided to face a jury the second time around.

Michael needed that one person to believe him. But maybe his odds would be better if he was looking for that one among twelve.

...

Eight women. Four men. Ten whites. Two blacks, of whom only one was male. That was the jury of Michael Evans's peers. During seven days of testimony, they had gotten to know one another, going to lunch in small groups, sharing polite smiles over morning coffee, becoming friendly in the way people do when sharing an extended inconvenience like jury duty.

Now it was Monday, April 25, 1977, and—after closing statements and their charging—the case was finally in their hands. Their first task was to select a foreperson, and they went with the woman who had become the obvious choice. Barbara Bartolotta was well-spoken and college educated, a natural leader who had been elected president of her high school class and just about every other group she had joined since then.

Now a forty-nine-year-old mother of five, she lived in Glenview, an affluent Cook County suburb. Her husband was an executive for Goldblatt's department store. She worked in the permissions and copyrights department for Scott Foresman, which published the Dick and Jane books. Before that, she had been a schoolteacher. Bartolotta seemed the perfect person to represent them during the unpleasant task ahead: deciding whether they could reach a unanimous decision about whether Michael Evans and his alleged accomplice, Paul Terry, were guilty of raping and killing Lisa.

Even in death, the little girl had been an aching presence throughout the trial. The photos of her body were on the back of the jurors' eyelids when they went to sleep. Her mother's testimony had been tearful and heart wrenching. Her loss was palpable. And it was the fervent hope of the prosecution it would remain so. Shortly after the jury began its deliberations, someone—Bartolotta doesn't remember who—walked into the jury room and set down the blood- and semen-stained clothing Lisa had been wearing when she was killed.

"They brought the scarves and clothing of this little girl right into the middle of the table and they just dumped it there," Bartolotta, now eighty-eight, recalled. "What the point of that was, I don't know. It was parked in the center of the table. Finally, one woman got so upset she just shoved them off in a corner somewhere. But they were in the middle of that table for a long time."

...

A few rooms away, Michael Evans's world had become very small. The holding cell where he was sent to await the verdict contained little more than a hard wooden bench for the hard men who sat there. In some ways, he still couldn't believe he was one of them. He had no criminal record. He had never been in any kind of trouble with the law. The only place he really struggled was in the classroom. In addition to his stutter, he had difficulty reading, something his illiterate mother couldn't help him with. He had recently left Chicago's Bowen High School to attend a vocational school. Beyond that, he was a cheerful sort—hence "Smiley"—a tall kid who loped along without much notice.

"I was just an ordinary boy," said Michael, now fifty-seven. "I played basketball. I played softball. I hung out with my homeboys in the neighborhood. I had an Afro. I wore these platform shoes. It was the seventies, you know?"

His family was originally from Mississippi, where they had picked cotton for generations. They came north in the 1950s, part of the Great Migration of African Americans fleeing the Jim Crow South for the hope of opportunity up north. His father was a custodian at a hotel. His mother was a homemaker and a devout attendee of a Southern Baptist church, where her son sang in the adult choir.

The Evanses had learned of Lisa Cabassa's death the same way everyone else in the neighborhood did. "We had watched it on the TV," Michael said. "Nothing like that had ever happened in our neighborhood before. It was a shock to all of us."

But, really, he hadn't thought much about it until that one morning six weeks later. He was walking with his six-year-old niece, Catherine, when that police van screeched to a halt next to him. He was taken to Area Two, where the detective squad was headed by Jon Burge, a man who did not let the law get in the way of his administration of justice. Federal lawsuits later revealed Burge and his detectives regularly submitted their presumed-guilty suspects to a variety of extreme interrogation tactics, including beatings, the use of cattle prods and simulated suffocation.

Michael was beyond overmatched. Already terrified after his rough ride in—and generally ignorant of his rights—he offered three different alibis for where he was at the time of the murder: in his cousin's basement; at 86th and Saginaw, with Catherine; at home with the flu. In truth, he didn't remember. To Michael Evans, January 14 had just been another Wednesday.

For more than twelve hours, a team of detectives hammered away at him, alternating between good cop and bad, offering him pizza, berating him, then giving him cigarettes. Finally, they put a confession in front of him and told him to sign it.

"I was so tired, I didn't know what I was signing," Michael said. "I didn't even read it. I was told if I signed it I could go home to my family, so that's what I did."

That the confession was thrown out before the first trial scarcely mattered. The police used it to book him. The prosecution used it to charge him.

Michael never did make it home to his family. He was taken to a juvenile facility and then, when he turned eighteen, he was transferred to the Cook County Jail.

"Being in the pit at the Cook County Jail, it was horrifying, even for one night," Michael said.

By the time of his second trial, he had been there for the better part of a year.

...

The jury room wasn't as unpleasant as Area Two or the Cook County Jail, not by any stretch. But it still wasn't a place where anyone relished spending time. The air conditioner spewed warm air. The water fountain—or "the bubbler," as Bartolotta called it—was located next to the toilet in the small bathroom, and it spit tepid water. The courthouse, a limestone monolith at the corner of 26th and California, had been built with towering columns that conveyed the majesty of justice to all who gazed upon it from the outside. The comfort of those inside was a secondary concern.

"The climate in that room, you had to have been there to understand," Bartolotta said. "It was just incredibly tense. You could cut the air with a knife. It was oppressive to even be in there."

As they made their first pass around the room and took a straw poll, it became clear the majority of the jury had already seen and heard enough. They voted eight to four to convict. A dead girl and a black defendant was enough for several of them.

"There were some openly prejudiced, openly bigoted people," Bartolotta said. "There was one woman who kept saying things like, 'Well, they all look alike.'"

Two other jurors, Bartolotta said, "lacked the intelligence to discuss anything rationally. They just thought Evans had to be guilty because he was there in court."

Even the lone black male juror thought Michael Evans was guilty. After the initial straw poll, two more jurors, eager to get the whole thing over with, switched over.

The only holdouts were Bartolotta and the black woman.

"It was tough going," Bartolotta said. "It was two of us against the rest of them."

...

There were no fingerprints tying Michael Evans to the crime. No blood samples. No footprints. And the first use of DNA evidence in a criminal trial was still a decade away. There was really only one reason Michael found himself in that cage at the Cook County Criminal Courthouse, and it was the eyewitness account of Judith Januszewski.

A married thirty-two-year-old of Polish heritage, she lived a few doors away from Michael. The neighborhood, once predominantly white, was in the midst of a tumultuous demographic shift. The Evanses had been the second black family on the block when they moved there in approximately 1970. Within a few years, it was more like fifty-fifty.

Januszewski worked as a secretary at Lamplighter Real Estate. Michael's friend also worked there. Michael said whenever he came to visit his friend at work, Januszewski was friendly to him, offering him cigarettes or coffee. Michael had wondered if she was flirting with him, but nothing ever came of it.

In the days after Lisa Cabassa's murder, as the city mourned and the police went on a rampage—arresting more than a dozen men in their fevered efforts—a man named Frank Martin, who ran the local Model Cities office, offered a reward for information about Lisa.

Januszewski soon appeared, telling Martin she had seen what she thought was a man dragging a girl into an alley on the night Lisa disappeared. Martin urged her to go to the police. At some point, after the medical examiner concluded more than one person would have been needed to subdue Lisa, Januszewski's account changed:

it was really two men pulling a young girl into an alley, where a third man was standing.

She said the men were "Negroes," in their late teens or early twenties. She described them to a sketch artist, but did not identify one of them as being Michael Evans, even though she had seen him around the neighborhood and in the real estate office many times.

Forty-one days after the crime—more than a month after she first went to Martin—Januszewski called the police, saying she wanted to "clear the air." They asked her to come into the precinct. There, Januszewski later testified, the detectives subjected her to an extended interrogation, denying her food and bathroom breaks, not allowing her to call her husband. She was under the impression she would not be permitted to leave until she made a statement.

That's when she first uttered the name Michael Evans.

The delay in her identification of Michael was soon explained with another story: She had been receiving phone calls, threatening her with rape and murder if she went to the police. The voice, she said, sounded like Michael's. She finally decided to approach the authorities when she found two .25-caliber bullets on her doorstep. A note was attached.

"The next time you talk to the police," it said, "you will get the real thing."

The police immediately placed a twenty-four-hour guard on Januszewski's house. She soon identified Paul

Terry, another kid from the neighborhood, as Michael's accomplice. After she agreed to testify against them, and in light of the threats she had received, the Illinois Law Enforcement Commission gave her $1,250—more than $5,000 in today's dollars—to help her move out of a neighborhood she couldn't wait to leave.

...

For Michael, there was a sense of betrayal when he learned Judy Januszewski had been the one to incriminate him. He had thought they were friends.

"Many nights, I laid in jail and I prayed God would touch her heart," Michael said. "I mean, how could she live with herself? How could she live with herself?"

Being forced to sit in court and listen to Januszewski describe him dragging Lisa Cabassa into an alley was similarly disorienting.

"The whole time, I'm thinking, 'What in the world is going on? How can this be happening in America, land of the free?' " Michael said. "I didn't think there was any way [the jury] could believe what she was talking about. The whole time I was telling Sam Adam, 'She's lying, she's lying.' "

Adam knew, of course. There were many flaws in Januszewski's statements, like the time problem. The Cabassas originally told police Lisa was last seen around 6:30 p.m. Any abduction had to have occurred within a few minutes of that, or else Lisa would have made it safely home. Yet time cards at the real estate office showed Januszewski didn't leave work until 8 p.m.

The problem was solved when Carmen Cabassa, Lisa's mother, changed her testimony. Adam didn't dare call her out on it, lest the jury turn on him for accusing a murdered girl's mother of lying. Besides, there were other issues he could bring out during his cross-examination, like the shifting number of suspects. First one. Then three. Or their size: Januszewski said the men she saw dragging Lisa into the alley were roughly the same height, about five feet eleven inches. Michael is six feet two inches. Paul Terry is five feet nine inches.

The descriptions she gave to the sketch artist were also inaccurate. But all of those discrepancies were explained, she testified, by her fear. Early on, she intentionally deceived the police because of the threats she was receiving.

"You were fooling them about telling them you didn't know who committed the crime?" Adam asked her.

"No, I wasn't fooling," she testified. "I was lying."

As for the sketch artist?

"I am telling the truth now," she testified, "and I was misleading the artist."

Adam kept Januszewski on the stand for four hours, trying to get her to admit she had made up everything in order to collect the reward, then layered one lie on top of another to cover for herself.

Januszewski wouldn't budge.

"I believe she had slept with the lie for so long, she

started to convince herself of it," Michael said. "She had started to believe maybe it was the truth."

...

For several members of the jury, Januszewski's steadfastness under cross-examination and her bravery—having the courage to testify after receiving such harrowing threats—overcame whatever doubts they might have had about her reliability.

"We all have had the same kind of fear," one female juror told the *Chicago Tribune*, declining to give her name for fear of retribution. "Sometime, something had happened to us that was so frightening we could visualize ourselves feeling the same way."

Barbara Bartolotta was less impressed by the state's star witness.

"To me, she was the most transparent type," Bartolotta said. "I could see right through her. She would sit there with her legs crossed and her bleached blonde hair. She just had a snippy air about her."

Still, Bartolotta couldn't make the other jurors see Januszewski the same way she did. She also couldn't get them to see the difficulty Michael would have had with the geography involved. It was two miles from where Lisa was last seen to where she was found. That was quite a distance for a boy who didn't have a driver's license and had never learned how to drive. He didn't have access to a car. He didn't even own a bike.

"It was just impossible to get from where he was to where they found the body in time," Bartolotta said. "But nobody seemed to want to listen to me when I said that."

After the first day of deliberation, the jury was sequestered at a nearby hotel. Bartolotta shared a room with the black female juror.

"I picked her as a roommate because I was afraid no one else would want to sleep with her and she'd get offended," Bartolotta said. "I remember something she told me. She told me the word from inside the jail was that [Michael Evans and Paul Terry] were innocent."

The next day, Tuesday, they continued deliberations. After several more hours—and with the two holdouts staying firm—they sent a note to Judge Frank Barbaro.

"We are deadlocked unalterably," it read. "What shall we do?"

Judge Barbaro sent a note back: "It is your duty to continue to deliberate."

...

Another night passed. Michael Evans went back to the pit at the county jail. The jury went back to the hotel.

On Wednesday morning, Michael returned to his courtroom-side cage and the jury returned to work. But by then, Bartolotta had lost her only ally.

"The black lady finally caved, so it was me against all of them," Bartolotta said. "They kept asking me, 'Barbara, what's wrong with you? What's wrong with you?' It was the women who were doing it. The men didn't say as much. . . . The exception was this one guy, he was a medical librarian at Resurrection Hospital. He kept telling me to use logic to come to a more sane conclusion."

Bartolotta thought she was using logic, of course. And so she continued to hold strong, insisting there was no chance she would change her mind.

The jury sent another note to Barbaro. "In almost four additional hours of deliberations we cannot reach a unanimous decision," it read.

Sam Adam immediately moved for a mistrial, telling his client that perhaps they had found the one person they had been looking for all along—and that it would lead to his freedom, if not immediately, then soon.

"He was positive if it came up for trial again he would beat it," Michael said. "He said he would blow 'em out of the water."

But Judge Barbaro denied the motion. This was already the second trial, and he didn't want to be the judge who made it necessary to have a third. He ordered the jury to continue to deliberate, forcing twelve exhausted people back into that hot, dingy room, which they increasingly viewed as their own temporary prison.

"The thinking was, 'We're not getting out of here until we reach a verdict,'" Bartolotta said. "That was made pretty clear to us."

The pressure on Bartolotta intensified. The jurors had already been sequestered for two nights. They had jobs and families to get back to. A woman with vacation plans worried she was going to miss her flight. Other jurors—who had once thought enough of Bartolotta to make her their foreperson—were now openly hostile to her.

An hour after Barbaro sent them back, Bartolotta relented.

"There's a saying, 'Forty million Frenchmen can't be out of step,'" Bartolotta said. "All these people thought one thing and eventually I started thinking, 'Well, there must be something wrong with me.' So finally I said I'd go along with them."

...

As he was led out of the cage and into the courtroom one final time, Michael Evans continued to believe there was one person—at least one person—who believed him.

"I thought for sure I'd be set free," he said. "What else could I think? I knew I was innocent."

He was wearing his best suit. His whole family was in the courtroom to support him, as they had been for the entire trial. He was ready to walk into their warm embrace after the hardest fourteen months of his life.

And then he heard the word: "Guilty."

"It's like my world came to an end," he said. "I could have fainted."

He turned toward his family. The look on his mother's face was sad and disgusted, he said. But there was something else there.

"My mother had this look she would give you where somehow you just knew she knew what she was doing—like 'there's a will, there's a way,'" Michael said. "And she looked at me like, 'Son, it's going to be okay.' I wanted to just melt. My mother was being strong for me, for the whole family."

At the next family gathering, she set a place at the table for Michael. It became a tradition that his sister—and, later, his niece—would call him and give him all the details of the meal, of what they had eaten and who said what, so he wouldn't feel like he had missed anything.

But the seat itself? That was empty.

It would stay that way for the next twenty-six years.

...

Clare and Catherine, Michael's family members, worked for decades as a mother-and-daughter team to prove Michael's innocence. Clare, who later took a job as a court clerk, eventually found medical records of a man who, on the day of Lisa Cabassa's death, entered Jackson Park Hospital at 6:46 p.m. He was released at 7:25 p.m., after being treated for wounds on his penis. Barbara Bartolotta said she continues to feel guilty about her inability to force a mistrial. She is now a regular donor to the Innocence Project. Her greatest regret, beyond Michael Evans's long incarceration, is that "whoever did it went free." Michael and his code-fendant, Paul Terry, filed civil rights lawsuits, which *are made very difficult because of immunity provided to those in the criminal justice system. Although less than a third of exonerees will receive a settlement or judgment of any kind, Paul Terry, who suffered profound mental damage behind bars, received $2.7 million. Michael Evans's attorney recommended taking his case to trial, where it was thought they could receive more. The jury returned a not guilty verdict against the police officers, and Michael received nothing. Nonetheless, he continues to smile. "I'm just glad to be free," he says.*

BRAD PARKS is the only author to have won the Shamus, Nero and Lefty awards, three of crime fiction's most prestigious prizes. A former journalist, Brad spent a dozen years with the *Washington Post* and the (Newark, New Jersey) *Star-Ledger*. He lives in Virginia with his wife and two school-age children.

Editors' Note

Incentivized informants—witnesses who are promised or given something in exchange for their testimony—are among the top six leading causes of wrongful conviction, according to the Innocence Project, contributing to the overturn of an estimated 15 percent of wrongful conviction cases with DNA testing evidence. Some informants work with the police and federal agents on a regular basis, receiving cash or a leniency deal made on another criminal case wherein the witness is involved. They are required to make their testimony persuasive in order to complete their end of the bargain. Whether the witness in Michael Evans's case had worked with the police before is unknown, but what is now clear is that the jury was never informed of the large cash reward she received.

Ken Wyniemko. Photo courtesy of Bruce Giffin

5.

DESCENT

ENTERING PRISON

Ken Wyniemko (Michigan exoneree), *as told to* Michael Harvey

---

FOR EVERY INNOCENT person, a prison sentence is a shattering experience. During the period before and during trial, the innocent is sustained by a hope that the terrible mistaken accusations will be refuted, justice will be served and innocence will prevail. Sentencing seems surreal, and then reality finally sinks in.

November 9, 1994. After the word "guilty," Ken Wyniemko's world goes dim. He can't feel his arms, legs, face or chest. Can't feel his heart beat or his eyes blink. Behind him his father sobs, pleading his son's innocence to anyone who'll listen. But no one's listening, least of all the state of Michigan.

Here come the sheriff's men with their belly chains

and shackles for hands and feet. They hustle Ken out from behind the defense table and past his parents, who reach out to touch his sleeve as he passes. And then Ken's gone, head down, doing the convict shuffle back to the prison van and a ride to Macomb County jail. Ken is forty-three years old, white and manages a bowling alley in Clinton Township, Michigan.

"I was John-Q average citizen. That's all I was. Worked all my life. Sometimes I worked two jobs. No criminal record. Just somebody going to work and trying to live a normal life."

"Normal" is over for Ken. Convicted on fifteen counts of sexual assault and other related charges, he's staring at forty years inside one of Michigan's maximum security lockups. Anyone who knows anything about the inside of a big-time prison will tell you—forget about the forty. With no survival skills and no friends inside, Ken's life is better measured in weeks, days, even minutes.

And so the ritual of descent begins.

Ken is transferred to the state pen two days after Christmas. On the day of his transfer, he's put in a holding cell in the county jail and allowed a phone call to his parents. His mother screams in the background as Ken explains to his dad what's about to happen. Ken's father has put his trust in the system, assuring his son that justice would prevail. And now it's come to this. Outside of Ken's cell, the sheriff's men are jingling their cuffs and their shackles. It's the sound of pure adrenaline, piss-pounding fear. Father and son pray together, then cry together. Ken's dad tells him to stay strong. Ken promises to do his best and hangs up.

Seven of them are chained together and herded into a prison van, tickets punched for Jackson prison—the state's oldest maximum security lockup. Ken doesn't have a strategy for surviving inside Jackson. Who does? The prison is reserved for Michigan's worst—rapists, murderers, drug dealers, gang bangers, con men, sadists and just plain evildoers. The truth is they'll either kill him or not. And there's not a fuck lot he can do about it. He keeps to himself on the ride out, tries not to make eye contact, barely feels a bump in the road. Ken hasn't done a thing. Nothing. The man is factually innocent of any crime. So why is he here? How is this happening?

April 30, 1994. A woman is brutally raped over several hours inside her home. A few months later, the victim mistakenly picks Ken out of a lineup. By itself, that's probably not enough to convince a jury to send a man with no criminal record to prison for the rest of his life. Police need more. And they're damn sure gonna get it. In the criminal justice system, it's called "sweetening the case." The sweetener this time is a snitch named Glen McCormick. He's looking down the barrel of a possible life stretch for multiple drug offenses when they stick him in the county lockup with Ken. After a day or two, a detective pulls McCormick out and takes him into an interro-

gation room. The detective offers what a Macomb County prosecutor would later call "the deal of the century"— the county will agree to a sentence of less than a year if McCormick testifies against Ken.

"I knew my past record would pretty much nail me to the ground," McCormick said. "I mean, at the time I was thinking, I'm trying to save my own hide."

McCormick is eager to cut a deal. There's only one problem—Ken hasn't said one word about the case. According to McCormick, the detective offers to "help out" with a copy of the police report.

"I'm sitting there in a six-by-six room with the detective," McCormick said. "He had the report in front of him. And he's sitting across from me. He asked me if I want a cup of coffee. I said yeah, so he gets up. When he got up he just turned the paper towards me. I mean, I'm not no dummy . . . I think I knew what he was trying to tell me to do."

After the detective has left the room, McCormick reads the report, memorizing details of the crime provided by the victim. When the detective returns, McCormick says he's ready to offer a statement about what Ken told him in the lockup. He then recites chapter and verse from the police report. In the parlance of lawyers it's called subornation of perjury. For Glen McCormick it's all about saving his own skin and just another part of the flesh-and-blood peddling that routinely goes on in our criminal justice system. At trial McCormick repeats his

performance on the witness stand. His testimony is more
than enough to secure a guilty verdict.

"I got on the stand and admitted that he did it,
knowing fully well that he didn't," McCormick said.

And that's how an innocent man like Ken
Wyniemko catches forty years in the state of Michigan.

Ken's van arrives at the gates of Jackson prison on the
afternoon of December 27, 1994. Processing into any
maximum security prison is designed to humiliate and
humble, to strip away any sense of individuality, dig-
nity or hope—all the things that get in the way of doing
"good time." Ken's indoctrination starts in the oldest part
of Jackson prison: Seven Block. The building is huge
and cold and barren and grim. Ken is stripped naked,
showered down with soap and water, then run through a
delousing station. He's issued clothes—three sets of prison
blues—and walks to a ramp that leads to the main block
of cells. Seven years after his release, I took the same walk
with Ken. We stood at the top of the ramp and peered
into the black maw of Seven Block. Ken told me about
that first day.

"You know when I first got here, I had met one of
the guards there. It was a lady and she had my file. She
looked at it and she said, 'Fifteen counts of rape. Fifteen
counts of rape? They're gonna have fun with, with your
ass in here.' I says, 'Ma'am, I didn't do it.' 'Yeah, that's
what everybody says.'"

Ken walks down the ramp and onto the main gallery. Several hundred men, locked in cages that run four stories high and a couple of football fields long, look down as the new arrivals are paraded before them.

"I was holding my two sets of blues, my prison uniform and towel as I was walking down that ramp," Ken said. "I was crying, I was crying and shaking, and as I walked down the floor to the stairwell to go up to the fourth gallery, guys were yelling, 'Fresh meat, fresh fish,' some guys blowing kisses."

The worst cells in any prison are the ones tucked up in the rafters. Smoke rises. Heat rises. All the smells of a prison live there. Those are the cells assigned to newbies. And Ken is as newbie as it gets. He's given a single cell, four flights up. Number 41-44. Ken takes a seat on the edge of his bunk. Fear slicks off the walls like sweat. The noise in his head builds until it's a blinding roar. Ken drops his face into his hands and begins to weep. A voice from the cell next door asks what's his problem. Ken tells the voice he doesn't belong here. This is a mistake. He's innocent. Someone has made a terrible mistake. His new neighbor laughs hard as hell and tells him that's what everyone says. Ken's voice is one of hundreds, thousands, whispering their tale to an audience that just doesn't give a damn.

Ken feels the bed sheet under his fingers and scratches at it. Then he begins to tear it into strips. Ken is in day one of a forty-year stretch and knows he's never gonna make it. So he decides to go out on his own terms. He ties the strips from the bed sheet together and starts to fashion a noose. He doesn't have much of a plan, but how much do you need? He'll wait until the lights go out and tie the sheets up high on the bars of his cell. Then he'll slip the noose around his neck and let himself drift up and away. Away from the prison, away from the noise and the smoke and the heat. Away from his forty years. To some better life. He'd already torn up about half the bed sheet when, for some reason he can't explain to this day, Ken stops and gets down on his knees in the middle of his cell.

"I got down on my knees. I started to pray and asking God for help. And I could feel, I can feel it now as I felt it that day on December 27th. I could feel like a hand touching my shoulder. And I heard a voice say, 'Kenny, you're gonna be okay.' "

A lot of people talk about religion, and everyone, it seems, has an opinion on the topic. But there's a difference between an opinion when you're sitting warm and comfortable and safe in your life and what Ken's sharing. When he looks at you and tells you he was touched on the shoulder in his cell, you know he believes it . . . and you can't help but feel it as well.

"I knew I wasn't gonna do forty years. I knew one day the truth would come out. I didn't know exactly how or when, but I knew that it would come out."

It will take the better part of a decade before that truth is made manifest, before Ken Wyniemko is freed and the real rapist is put behind bars.

77

...

In January 2003, evidence still existed that could be subjected to DNA testing. The tests revealed that another man who had already been arrested multiple times on sex-related offenses had committed the rape. On the day of his release, Ken made time to visit the grave of his father, who had died three years earlier. "I got down on my knees and I brushed the leaves off his headstone and I kissed his headstone and I said, 'Dad, I made it home. I made it home, Dad.'" Today Ken travels around the country, telling his story and explaining how innocent people can and do go to jail.

———

MICHAEL HARVEY is a writer, journalist and documentary producer. He is the best-selling author of seven crime novels: *The Chicago Way, The Fifth Floor, The Third Rail, We All Fall Down, The Innocence Game, The Governor's Wife* and *Brighton.*

Editors' Note

In 2013, the United States led the world in the number of incarcerations. Not only did American prisons hold more than 2,220,000 individuals, more than any other nation and almost 25 percent of the total number of prisoners in the world, the portion of its population imprisoned was the highest in the world, at over 0.7 percent, or 700 people in every 100,000. The Bureau of Justice Statistics (BJS) estimates that 6.6 percent of all individuals born in the United States each year will spend some time in prison. However, this is not because of a rise in violent crime; rather, it is primarily the result of a "tough-on-crime" attitude taken by legislators and law enforcement officials. According to the BJS, at the end of 2013, 47 percent of prisoners in state and federal prisons with a sentence of a year or more are serving time for a nonviolent offense.

The greatest challenge facing the American justice system is overcrowding. Between 1979 and 2009, the number of prisoners in state and federal facilities increased almost 430 percent. Since 1980, the federal prison population has grown 721 percent, and in the last twenty-nine years, the state prison population has grown over 240 percent. In 2014, nineteen states and the Federal Bureau of Prisons were operating their prisons at more than 100 percent capacity, with states like Illinois at 171 percent, California at 136 percent, and Ohio and Wisconsin each over 131 percent. The results of overcrowding are often devastating: High costs result in poor quality of food; sanitation is often abysmal.[1] Human Rights Watch, an inter-

---

1   In a survey of 1,788 male inmates in Midwestern prisons reported in *The Prison Journal* in 2000, about 21 percent responded they had been coerced or pressured into sexual activity during their incarceration, and 7 percent that they had been raped in their current facility.

national organization devoted to fighting human rights abuses, stated: "Jail and prison conditions are in many respects unsafe and inhumane."[2] According to BJS surveys, 4,309 inmates died in state or local prisons in 2012, most from illness (though the leading cause of death in local jails is suicide).

---

2   https://www.hrw.org/united-states/criminal-justice.

Kirk Bloodsworth

Chapter 6

THE FORTUNE COOKIE

THE LESSONS LEARNED

Kirk Bloodsworth (Maryland exoneree),
as told to **Lee Child**

———

THE MARINE CORPS motto is "Semper fidelis,"
always faithful—to the Marines, to the government of
the United States, to the principles on which the United
States is founded. For ex-Marine Kirk Bloodsworth,
however, "Semper fi" became a personal mantra,
reminding him to be faithful to himself and to believe
in himself when everyone around him had lost hope. It
became the armor that allowed him to survive an eight-
year journey through hell.

"If this can happen to an honorably discharged Marine
with no criminal history, it can happen to anybody."

...

You step into a small metal box set on a slate floor inside a one-hundred-year-old Gothic castle with stone walls twenty feet thick. You're not a tall man but the box makes a room so cramped you can put your palms on both opposing sides at once. Front to back is three short, shuffling steps. The room stinks. There's a metal toilet. You're allowed to flush it once a day. Sometimes twice. It has a washbasin dished into the top of the tank. There's a thin damp mattress with unexplained stains. All day and all night you hear the scurrying and scuttling of rats and mice. You learn to sleep with toilet paper wadded in your ears to keep the roaches out.

This is your home until the day you die.

Literally.

You're on death row.

The guards open the windows wide in the wintertime and keep them closed tight in the summer. They let you shower once every two weeks. Just for the extra torment. Because you deserve it. You raped a nine-year-old girl. Then you strangled her, and when that didn't kill her, you pulped her head with a rock. Nine years old. A child. You destroyed her.

Except you didn't.

You're completely innocent.

You never saw the girl. You were never in her neighborhood. You have five alibi witnesses who say so. You look nothing like the police sketch.

But no one will listen to you.

Your name is Kirk Bloodsworth, and they're going to kill you for something you didn't do. When the verdict came in at your trial, the courtroom erupted in applause. You heard someone shout, "Give him the gas and kill his ass."

You sit on the edge of your filthy bed with your hands on your knees, and you stare at the floor.

How did this happen?

...

Thirty-one years later, in the dining room of his small but pretty house near Philadelphia, Kirk says, with considerable understatement, "Withstanding captivity was tough. It was a bad place. I hated every minute. Guys were getting stabbed over arguments about snack biscuits and cans of soda. Guys were killing themselves. One guy I knew stuck pencils through his eyes. One of my friends hung himself, the day after telling his mother he didn't want to see her anymore."

Kirk uses the word "captivity," rather than "prison" or "being locked up" because military terminology comes naturally to him; he's a former Marine. And indeed, he used his Marine training to survive. He completed the POW course at Camp Lejeune, where the Corps had a faux gulag, realistic in every detail, with Russian-speaking guards. The pressure sent some guys nuts. But, he says, "One of the instructors was an old guy, a Vietnam vet, who survived nine years in one of their most brutal prisons. He lost an arm through being bound, like John McCain. He told us he got through with a kind of meditation. He loved Triumph motorcycles, and he would imagine taking one apart, cleaning the pistons, oiling the components, putting it all back together, over and over again. That's what I did. I would sit on the floor and go crabbing. I got so good at it I swear I could hear the water lapping at my boat. That gave me peace. I left that place so many times in my mind."

He talks with the short, flat, slightly nasal vowel sounds of rural Maryland and southern Pennsylvania, strangely similar to the vowel sounds of my own childhood, three thousand miles east, in Birmingham, England. "Might" and "night" become "moit" and "noit," and "quite" and "like" become "quoit" and "loik." He says, "There was one rapist who boasted about his conquests. I told him if he talked to me again I would beat him to death with his shoe."

I ask him about the moment after the arrest, and the investigation, and the trial, and the conviction, and the sentence, when the cage door slammed shut and the lock turned. Did he despair? "Not for one minute," he replies. "I never gave up. I knew I would get out. I didn't know how. But I was relying on the one thing they could never take away from me—I was an innocent man. That was my cloak. How does a man accused of killing a nine-year-old girl go out in the population on his own? While I was there they had one of the biggest riots in the penitentiary for thirty years, and I walked through it like they didn't see me. Like I was wearing an invincible cloak. I started a letter-writing campaign. I wrote letters all day every day until my hands hurt. I wrote all kinds of people. I wrote Ronald Reagan, and all kinds of musicians and authors and stars of the screen. None of them ever wrote back."

I pause for a moment, suddenly ashamed about the letters I have ignored.

Then like all good storytellers, Kirk starts back at the beginning.

...

He says, "I had a wonderful childhood. I grew up in a small town on the eastern shore of Maryland, full of fish-ermen and crabbers. We rode our bicycles until two or three in the morning, we were fishing on a body of water seven miles across, all by ourselves, catching crabs. I had a trap line for muskrats, and I'd check it every day. My father took me hunting. We had a big dinner on Sunday. We went to see my grandparents. We always checked in on family. If you were to make a picture of me growing up, it would have been a Norman Rockwell painting."

With a touch of the Artful Dodger, I think to myself, and a soundtrack by Jimi Hendrix, because he continues, "We ate fish and steamed crabs and drank beer and chased women and smoked weed. By the time I was thirteen or fourteen it was everywhere. I loved weed and women and beer and parties. That was my thing. Saturday night was all we had to look forward to. Because we worked so hard. In the middle of everything else we'd be looking for raccoon—in 1976 that was thirty, forty bucks, right there, walking right past you. Everyone had a hustle. We would swim under boats and cut ropes off the wheels and make twenty bucks a time. In the summer you'd go right down the line. An enterprising guy who could hold his breath and didn't mind to get wet could make a hundred dollars."

Then his face sets, sad, because now he's speaking of the dead: "My father was a fierce worker. My mother too. She was the giant in the household. She wanted me to get an education. She didn't want me to talk like a turnip farmer. She was smart herself. She could do the *New York Times* crossword puzzle in twenty minutes. She read all kinds of books. She was hard on me. She was stern. She hated a loafer. Consequently neither my sister nor I was a loafer."

I ask what he remembers of the wider world at the time—Vietnam, maybe, and Watergate. He answers, "I remember Richard Nixon on the TV. I never trusted that man. My mother said he was a lying SOB. You would see the flag-draped coffins coming in. It was awful. But my father was very patriotic. He had been a Marine. He talked about the Corps like it was heaven on earth. When I finished boot camp I told him he was a liar. But the good thing was my mother had been more of a drill sergeant than any of those cats. The more they would yell at me the more into it I got. It was a perfect marriage, really. I was seventeen. I went in a year early. It was the first time I ever raised my voice to my mother. She didn't want to sign the papers. She thought they were going to send me to war and kill my ass. It was 1978, and she'd been through Vietnam as an adult. But I slapped my hand down on the table and said I was joining. And the recruiter was standing right there."

Then his face changes again, reflective, almost confessional, and he says, "But the Marine Corps never lived up to my expectations. I didn't like half the people. Because they were assholes. The boys that die are following some asshole who's keeping his friends alive. And I didn't know if I could kill somebody. That was a thing too. I remember Muhammad Ali speaking out about that crap. I didn't know if I could pull the trigger on a person. I could shoot a duck in a minute, because I was going to eat it. But I didn't know why I was shooting at a target shaped like a man."

Then he waves off his doubts and brightens. "I was on the track team for the Marines. I threw the discus. That was the thing that changed my life. I had the best coach in the world—an Olympian himself. But the military itself never suited me. I rebelled against it quite a bit. I just thought they were a little too much. I did four years active duty and two years reserve. They tried to sign me up for another tour, but I had punched a lieutenant in the head. We were doing a live fire exercise. The deal was, when the red smoke popped, you would shift your fire to the right. The lieutenant was new, straight out of the Naval Academy, and he was firing downrange, and the red smoke popped, and I tapped him on the helmet and suggested he shift right, but he shifted left instead, telling me not to tell him what to do, and he was all *rat-a-tat*, and I'm shouting stop, stop, and I hit him between the ear and the lower mandible. He rolled over pretty easily. But I got in big trouble. They never liked me after that."

He sweeps his blunt hands across the table, as if clearing imaginary crumbs, the end of one thing and the start of the next. He says, "I went back to Maryland, trying to save up enough money to buy my own boat. But it was tough. Boats were getting very expensive. I wanted fiberglass so I wouldn't have to worry about the wood. But I didn't have a hundred thousand dollars. So I knew a guy whose helper had quit. A hard man, a crabber, well-known in the area. Old-school. He brought his lunch in a pail. I signed on with him. He kept his boat pristine clean. I remember when we were baiting with herring . . . their scales are the stickiest thing on the planet. You have to scrape them off or they bond to the wood. It's a pain. But I was in good shape, twenty-three years old, working all day, going out at night, having some fun."

Then he pauses. He says, "That's when I met Wanda, my first wife."

He pauses again. Says, "And that's when it all started to go south."

...

Kirk takes a deep breath, and continues, "Wanda was ten years older than me. She was a party girl. I liked to party too, but you had to go to work. That's how it was. Whether you were high or whatever, you worked the next day. Wanda would disappear for a couple of days at a time. I don't know if there was infidelity. But there were mishaps all the time. She wrecked my car. She was drinking a lot of Jack Daniel's. Eventually I had enough. I said, 'Go back to Baltimore so I can work without having to worry about you.' I got my uncle to give me ten bucks and I put her on the bus. But I missed her. I pined over her for two weeks."

Then he stops, and takes a breath, and prepares to make what I infer will be a central point. He says, "Now I'm going to back up and tell you a story about the day we got married. April of 1984. I'm driving to the wedding. I'm going across the big bay bridge that goes from Maryland across the Chesapeake to Baltimore. I'm starving. I haven't eaten anything since the night before. It's 11:30, and the wedding is at 1. I'm looking around the car, trying to find a bag of chips or a packet of crackers or something. But all I find is a fortune cookie. I grab that thing and rip it open and drop the fortune and eat the cookie. Then the traffic slows up in the center of the span and I look down and read the fortune. It says, 'Turn Around.' "

...

Kirk is quiet for a moment, and says, "I didn't turn around. I never paid attention to crap like that. But I had an ominous feeling. I could have turned around. I could have hit the ramp at the end of the bridge and gone back the other way. But I didn't. I had a ring from the pawn shop, twenty-five dollars. My mother didn't come to the ceremony. She hated Wanda. But my dad showed up. He had a suit on. He gave me two hundred bucks in my hand, and said, 'I hope you know what you're doing.'"

He pauses again, clearly answering his father's ancient question in his mind, for the hundredth time. Or the thousandth. In the negative, presumably. He says, "On the honeymoon I broke my tooth, chewing on a champagne cork. Wanda had a missing tooth on the other side, so now we were a pair."

Then he takes it up again where he had left off, ten bucks from his uncle, Wanda on the bus to Baltimore, missing her, pining for her. He says, "I hitchhiked down there. I'll never forget it. I was thinking about the fortune cookie again. I walked right into it."

...

He takes another breath, the memories inevitably vivid, even thirty-one years later. His life about to change. He says, "We ended up staying at her sister's. It was a flop-house, basically. Wanda, me, her sister, a brother-in-law, a couple of their friends. Not very savory by society's stan-

THE FORTUNE COOKIE: THE LESSONS LEARNED

dards. Not very popular with the neighbors. I got a job very fast, at the Wicker Warehouse. In the meantime, a little girl called Dawn Hamilton was found killed, not far from that place. Maybe a couple miles, as the crow flies. About three miles from where we were living. July 25th, 1984. It was my day off. They had it on the TV news. The police had a sketch of a man, from two little boys, aged eight and ten. They had seen Dawn Hamilton walking with a man. I found out later they had just caught a turtle. They were looking up at a man in an elevated position. They said he was six feet five. The police made a picture. It looked nothing like me. Looked nothing like anybody. And eventually nineteen years later when they got the right guy he turned out not to be six feet five but five feet six. A little sawn-off thing."

Then he stops, his blunt hands sweeping imaginary crumbs again. The start of a nightmare. He says, "A neighbor called the police and said I was the guy in the sketch. Revenge, presumably, for dirtying up the neighborhood with the flophouse."

...

At that point Kirk was arrested. In retrospect it is hard to overestimate the outrage felt at the time by the community over such a brutal, disgusting, heinous crime. Ironically, no one felt it more than Kirk himself. He says, "I was mad at the nature of the crime—this girl was just destroyed. How a person could do that to someone—let alone a child—just infuriated me. So I was sticking up for myself. I was indignant. How could they think I could do something like that? How the hell? I wanted to beat the crap out of those cops. I wanted to slap the shit out of them. They were wasting time. The real guy was in the wind. So I was fighting back. And I guess that pissed them off."

And of course in retrospect it is hard to overestimate the intense pressure the cops were under to solve the crime. They had to get a guy. Kirk was a little late to understand it didn't have to be the right guy. Any guy would do. Such a sentiment was outside his frame of reference. He was raised right. He was a Marine. He was a discus champion. He worked hard. He scraped every last herring scale off the wood. His personal standards were very high.

But soon enough he felt the railcar start to roll. He says, "They had a hard-on for me. They wanted to believe it. They were fitting me in. They were rolling me up into a cigar and lighting the match."

He calmed down and got serious.

"Which was a mistake," he says. "The more I talked, the worse it got. I should have stayed pissed off. I should never have done that unemotional crap they tell you to do."

They wanted to test his shoe. He says, "But I couldn't let them, because I had pot in my shoe. A little baggie. They said I looked nervous, which I was, because of the pot. All that was against me. They asked me how come

I knew about the rock used to stove in her head? I said, 'Because you showed it to me!' The panties, too. They were giving me information about the crime, and then finding it suspicious that I knew."

Thirty-one years later, in his dining room, I ask him when he knew for sure he was in trouble. He says, "When they took me out of the room where they had been questioning me and stuck me in a holding cell. It was six in the morning, and already hot. Eighty-plus degrees, before the sun even came up. That was one hot-ass summer. I went into some sort of protection mode. I didn't come out of it for nine years. Like guard duty in the Corps. Sleeping while you're awake. I was asleep, but I was listening. I heard them say, 'How can he sleep after doing what he did to that girl?' They coached the two little boys. The eight-year-old didn't know any-thing. They told him to agree with whatever the ten-year-old said. Even so they didn't pick me out of the lineup. But two weeks later their parents called and said the kids had made a mistake and now they were sure it was number six. Which had been me. After my face being all over the TV for two weeks. I was getting fed a shit sandwich. There was nothing I could do. I felt help-less, where previously I could always help myself. I felt I was caught up in a massive human lottery of some sort. I'm no angel, I was born on Halloween, and my name is Bloodsworth. What chance did I have? What could I do? Sometimes early on I sensed they had doubts, but they didn't want to admit they made a mistake. They would rather I died. I got the sense it was like a covert military action. Expendables had to go. I was collateral damage, for the sake of their public reputation."

He sweeps imaginary crumbs again. Investigation over. On to the trial. He says, "I had five eyewitnesses who said I was nowhere near. That the boys were wrong. But it's about who tells the story. Mine were family and friends. What else were they going to say? Whereas what ax did the boys have to grind? The jury didn't know they had been manipulated. I had a little bit of hope while I was waiting for the verdict to come back. Two hours is all they took. And they said guilty, and I thought, *Oh man, this is bullshit.* I thought I was going to die."

...

Then came the penitentiary, and the letter writing, and the stabbings, and the suicides, and a cracked skull from an attack with a sock full of batteries. He says, "The worst thing was my mother died before I got out. I talked to her two days before. She always knew I didn't do it. She knew her own kids. A mother always does. They didn't let me go to her funeral."

But as well as writing letters, Kirk was reading. Books, journals, scientific papers. In the 1980s, DNA was a brand new thing. Kirk made himself an expert, in the obsessive way only a man in prison can. He got hopeful. "But they said the physical evidence from my case was gone. It was lost. No one knew where it was. In the end they said it had been inadvertently destroyed. I was locked up, and now it felt like they had thrown away the key. But one day my lawyer was at the courthouse, and he knew one of the bailiffs, because he was there a lot, and the guy asked, 'What are you looking for?' And my lawyer said, 'the Hamilton evidence from the Bloodsworth case.' And the guy said, 'Oh, that's in the judge's closet. In a paper bag in a cardboard box.' And it was. Just dumped in there. They recovered half a cell from it. Which is very damn small in the scheme of things. And the DNA proved I didn't do it."

I ask how he had felt at that moment. The answer is not as triumphant as I expected. The measure of Kirk Bloodsworth as a man is that his quest for justice was as much on behalf of Dawn Hamilton as himself. The nine-year-old girl. The victim. He says, "I never forgot her. I felt really bad for her. I was fighting for her, partly. My mother always said, 'If you don't stand for something, you'll fall for anything.' Everyone else had forgotten her. I wanted them to get the right guy."

Which they didn't, not for another ten years, by which time DNA databases had been established. Eventually a hit came up. The little sawn-off guy. Five feet six, not six feet five, and facially nothing at all like the composite sketch the Baltimore police had gotten from the two little boys. By an amazing coincidence Kirk had met him in prison, where the guy was serving time for another offense. Kirk says, "Looking back, I realize the guy was kind of quiet around me. Kind of squirrelly. I guess I would have killed him if I knew."

No angel.

...

Thirty-one years later we sit in the dining room of the quiet, pleasant house. Kirk Bloodsworth is the first person ever exonerated from death row by postconviction DNA testing. As such, he has grown into an elder statesman role. He has testified before Congress and acted as a go-to spokesperson on numerous occasions in many contexts. Richard Branson flew him to London to present a life-time achievement award to the scientist who pioneered the techniques. He is well-read and well-informed. No longer the scrappy shore kid he once was. He doesn't talk like a turnip farmer. As a hobby he makes exquisite silver jewelry. He shows me his basement workshop. He gives me a tiny silver box made in the shape of a book. He tells me he quit smoking eight months ago. He tells me he still enjoys weed. We agree there's nothing wrong with that. "Although," he says, "I did way more drugs in prison than I do out in the world."

We talk about lessons learned. He feels that public expectations about DNA testing make the police far more honest than they were. Not that he hates cops. He likes them, for the most part. He knows that without them we'd pretty soon be living in a postapocalyptic vision of hell. But he knows emotions can run high. When torn and bloodied and pulped nine-year-old corpses turn up in small towns like Baltimore, all bets are off. Any guy will do. But DNA is impartial. Scientific, not emotional. Not that experts are always what they seem. We talk about a ballistics guy who testified at a lot of criminal trials, who turned out not to be an expert at all. His so-called qualifications were all made up. Before he was exposed, his testimony sent seventeen people to death row. Many of those seventeen can't be released now, because they were executed long ago.

We talk about the unreliability of eyewitness testimony. The final frontier, somehow, in tandem with DNA. So human, so obvious. We all know what we saw. We all know what happened right in front of our own eyes. Except we don't. What seems to be the best type of evidence is very often the weakest. Getting people to accept that will be a huge task.

I ask him how many innocent people he thinks are in prison right now. He quotes a figure of 154 so far released from death row alone. He says innocence projects are quite rightly cautious and conservative. They can't afford blunders. So the true number of innocent people scheduled to die is probably far higher. Ten percent, maybe? He should know. He's been through it. The American prison population is 2.3 million. Which at the same percentage would mean 230,000 people are suffering for no reason. Nearly a quarter of a million innocent men and women, sitting on the edge of their filthy cots, their hands on their knees, staring at the floor, thinking, *How did this happen to me?*

...

The state of Maryland paid Kirk Bloodsworth $300,000 for lost income. The Kirk Bloodsworth Postconviction DNA Testing Program was established under the 2004 Innocence Protection Act, providing funding for testing, encouraging states to preserve evidence and make DNA testing available for inmates seeking to prove their innocence. Kirk previously served as a program officer for the Justice Project in Washington, D.C., and is an activist against the death penalty. His story is told in more detail in Bloodsworth: The True Story of the First Death Row Inmate Exonerated by DNA *by Tim Junkin, and a documentary by Gregory Bayne,* Bloodsworth: An Innocent Man.

LEE CHILD is a British crime writer, the author of twenty novels about former American military policeman Jack Reacher. Despite selling millions of copies, Lee announced his intentions many years ago to stop with twenty-one books. He is copresident of the International Thriller Writers and former president of Mystery Writers of America. Lee was given the Lifetime Achievement Award of the Crime Writers Association in 2013.

Editors' Note

Notwithstanding the prevalence of DNA testing as a forensic tool in televised crime dramas, DNA-based exonerations are not yet the dominant part of the overall number of exonerations. According to the National Registry, in 1989, 2 out of 22 exonerations (9 percent) were DNA related. In 2009, 29 out of 89 (32.5 percent) were DNA based, but by 2015, that rate had flattened to 26 out of 156 exonerations (16.7 percent). Overall, DNA evidence was a factor in just over 24 percent of the exonerations.

Certainly, a significant hurdle to increased use of DNA testing is the inadequacy of crime labs in the United States. According to the Bureau of Justice Statistics, there were 411 publicly funded labs in 2009. At the end of 2009, the surveyed labs reported a backlog of *over one million requests*, most of which were forensic DNA testing.

Audrey Edmunds

7.

A STUDY IN SISYPHUS

SERVING TIME

Audrey Edmunds (Wisconsin exoneree), *as told to* **Judge John Sheldon and Gayle Lynds**

———

HOW DO YOU prove that you didn't commit a crime when there were no witnesses against you, just an unexplained dead baby? How do you live with the knowledge that the courts have labeled you a "child murderer," because someone must have killed the child? How do you keep hope alive, when every time you push the rock uphill, it rolls back down to the bottom, and you have to start all over to convince the world of your innocence?

August 2007. A tall woman with long auburn hair leaves a small room and enters a hallway at the John C. Burke Correctional Center in Waupun, Wisconsin. She's dressed in a pea-green uniform resembling pajamas. The hallway's concrete walls are painted off-white, its concrete ceiling white. The floor is green linoleum. There are no windows, no wall hangings, no furniture. Fluorescent lights, recessed into the ceiling, offer the only illumination.

The woman's name is Audrey Edmunds. She has been in prison for ten and a half years for murder.

Now she's going to a hearing with an officer of the state's parole board. She's done this twice before, unsuccessfully. Other prisoners have told her that the officials won't grant parole until a prisoner reaches her "mandatory release date"—two-thirds of the original sentence. For Audrey, that's a year and a half away. Moreover, to get parole she'd have to admit that she committed the crime. No chance of that.

But she's required to attend the meeting anyway. Besides, there's always hope. And need: Her children are growing up without her. She was imprisoned two days after her youngest daughter's first birthday. Agony from that appalling abandonment has never left her.

At the end of the corridor, Audrey turns left. She passes through a doorway into a large room where the prisoners eat. This room also serves as the visitors' area. In a far corner, Audrey sees three people at a table talking, one dressed in a uniform identical to her own. It's another inmate, Sally, who's doing a ten-year sentence for possession of heroin. Sally has told Audrey that, on balance, she prefers being "inside," because she's safer, gets fed and doesn't get cold in the winter. Audrey doesn't know whether to pity her for what she doesn't have—children and a home awaiting her come to mind first—or to envy her because she can tolerate what to Audrey has been over a decade of horror.

...

WAUNAKEE, WISCONSIN

October 1995–February 1997. In the fall of 1995 Audrey was a middle-class, stay-at-home mom in Waunakee. She and her husband Dave were raising two daughters, ages four and two, in a comfortable three-bedroom ranch. Audrey was expecting a third child in early 1996. Dave worked for a rock quarrying business, and he'd recently been promoted to the company's St. Paul, Minnesota, office. Since that was about 250 miles away, they'd sold their home and were preparing to move.

They first came to Waunakee after their oldest child, Carrie, was born. The neighborhood they settled in was perfect for young parents. Just take your children outdoors and they'd start playing with the neighborhood kids and pretty soon you'd be following them into somebody's yard, or they'd be coming into yours. There were church events, barbecues, parties in front of someone's TV to watch a football game and dinners at friends' homes. Their lives in Waunakee were fulfilling and fun.

Leaving would be sad, but Audrey and Dave were looking forward to a new city, a new job and settling among
new friends.

To bring in extra money, Audrey was providing
part-time day care for friends and neighbors, taking in
up to three children besides her own. In October 1995,
a mother delivered her seven-month-old daughter for the
day. Natalie was crying when she arrived and hadn't taken
her formula that morning. She finally quieted down when
Audrey settled the child in a baby carrier in one of her
bedrooms. When she checked several minutes later, however, Natalie was limp and not breathing. Frantic, Audrey
dialed 911 for help and then followed the dispatcher's
instructions for infant CPR. The police came quickly, and
a Med Flight helicopter landed in the backyard to rush
Natalie to a Madison hospital. She died that night.

The baby's symptoms included cranial bleeding and
bleeding behind the eyes. This, the medical authorities
decided, meant Audrey must have shaken the baby violently and caused her death—"shaken baby syndrome,"
they called it. Audrey was charged with first-degree
reckless homicide. At trial, medical experts testified that
shaken baby syndrome established to "a medical cer-
tainty" that Audrey had murdered the child, and she was
convicted. On February 20, 1997, she began serving an
eighteen-year sentence.

...

TAYCHEEDAH CORRECTIONAL INSTITUTION
FOND DU LAC, WISCONSIN

March 1997—three weeks later. Audrey awoke. She guessed it was after midnight, but she had no way of knowing the time because all her personal belongings, including her eyeglasses and watch, had been confiscated when she'd first been locked up.

It was the noise of jangling keys, like a rattling of light chains, that awakened her. Guards were approaching the direction of her cell. Their noise signaled humiliation, perhaps worse. Whatever they intended, it wasn't going to be gentle—no chance, not prison guards, not in maximum security, not in the middle of the night. Audrey waited, anxiety increasing.

The sound stopped just outside her door, followed by the metallic noises of a key inserted in the lock, the key turning, the lock responding. From the bunk overhead she heard her cell mate's worried breathing. The light in the cell went on.

Fear boiled up from Audrey's midsection as the heavy door squealed open. She was trapped, surrounded by concrete walls and the iron bunk above, nowhere to go, no way to hide. Two guards—always two of them—tough women, and no security cameras in her cell to deter them. Audrey sat up in her bunk and shrank against the wall.

One guard stood in the doorway as the other entered.

"Kepler," the guard in the room said, "UA time." Urine analysis.

The bile in Audrey's throat subsided. Her cell mate, Gloria Kepler, had had a visitor that afternoon, her lawyer. Lawyer or not, the guards were checking to see whether he'd slipped her drugs. If so, she'd probably have taken them; traces would be found in her urine.

"Get out of your bunk," the guard ordered. She snapped on latex gloves.

Audrey watched Gloria's thin legs slide down from the bunk above. Gloria put a foot onto Audrey's bunk and lowered herself to the floor.

The guard handed Gloria a plastic container. "Piss into the cup," she ordered.

Taking the cup, Gloria stepped to the metal toilet attached to the rear wall. She dropped her underwear to her ankles, sat on the toilet, positioned the cup and urinated. The sound of the liquid hitting the hard plastic container was harsh, the smell of urine sharp.

Gloria returned the cup to the guard, who screwed a cover onto it and left. The other guard shut the door, locked it and turned off the light from a switch in the hallway.

The jangling keys receded. In the dark, Audrey heard the sound of Gloria redressing, then felt her step onto Audrey's vinyl-covered foam mattress as she climbed into her bunk. Neither said anything.

Audrey lay back down and crossed her arms on her forehead as the uncontrollable, endless cycle of emotions started again: fear of the guards turned into anger at them, which triggered anger at how the prosecutor had attacked her at trial, which recalled her disbelief at the verdict, and the pain of public disgrace, and how unjust the punishment was, and the horror of losing her family, missing Dave, heartache for her children, despair that her prison time was passing so slowly, outrage at the judicial system, anger at the guards, resentment of the prosecutor, disbelief, pain, victimization, horror, loneliness, heartache, despair . . . and on, and on, and over again. Relentless, irrepressible and self-igniting anguish.

She managed to interrupt the torment by forcing herself to concentrate on hope: Her lawyers would soon file a motion for a new trial. They were enthusiastic; many prejudicial mistakes had occurred during the trial. Foremost was the trial judge's refusal to allow the testimony of witnesses who'd observed that Natalie's parents had displayed an "odd lack of panic" and a "very limited expression of grief" at the hospital just before Natalie died. That meant the jury's attention had been drawn to the wrong issue: The question they should have considered was not *whether* Natalie had been shaken violently, but *who* had done it. This evidence was crucial to the defense and to finding the truth, the lawyers said, and its exclusion entitled her to a retrial.

Hope was the best anesthetic for Audrey's wheeling emotions.

...

July 1998—one year, four months later. After months of filings, legal memoranda, reply memoranda, argument and consideration, Audrey learned the trial judge denied her motion for a new trial.

Audrey was sickened by the news, not only because the motion had failed but also because it meant more time in maximum security. Hour after hour, day after day and week after week, Audrey had to sit with her cell mate "in our tiny closet of a room, staring at the walls." Such tedium froze the passage of time and invited the emotional loop to keep running through her mind.

The noise in the place only worsened her emotional turmoil. Besides the wailing and screaming of angry or deranged prisoners, there were prisoners yelling to others in nearby cells, through the metal doors or out the windows. Then there were the guards, bellowing to or at prisoners.

There was no air circulation—you could open the little cell window only two inches. She sweated in the summer—the concrete was uninsulated and fans weren't permitted—and shivered in the winter. The stench of bodily functions was inescapable: lying in her bunk while her cell mate with diarrhea sat on the toilet three feet from her pillow. No air fresheners were allowed.

Respite from this claustrophobic bedlam was only occasional. Meals three times a day, but they had just fifteen minutes to gobble their food. She could exercise two or three times a week in the gym, provided there was adequate staff—always an uncertainty. A visit to the library a few times a week. Audrey and her cell mate were allowed a thirteen-inch television and a small radio. They could stare out their one-by-two-foot window at a parking lot and a guard tower. The only thing to look forward to each day was when Audrey could phone Dave and the kids—for fifteen minutes, if she were allowed to.

Audrey grew desperate for anything to get her out of her concrete box. A job would do it. Her first assignment, cleaning latrines, was a relief. In the winter they'd let her shovel snow. For a while she painted the ceiling of the gymnasium. Working in the kitchen was best, because the staff was respectful and trusting—they had to be, considering the knives scattered throughout the place. Audrey cherished the respect and the comparative quiet there. All of these jobs paid one dollar a day, but the issue wasn't income, it was sanity.

Visitors, of course, were the high point of the week. Friday afternoons Audrey would wait by her cell window, watching for her family to arrive. She'd see Dave drive up and park, then open the car doors; the kids would pile out and run happily up the sidewalk to the prison entrance. For them this wasn't prison, it was a place to visit Mommy, and they loved it, and so did Audrey. Traveling here was difficult: an eight-hour round trip from the Twin Cities, hard enough for the kids, especially tough and expensive for Dave. And for Audrey, the hours after they left were wretched, empty.

Yet her lawyers gave her more hope: They had filed an appeal of the judge's order denying the motion for a new trial. The lawyers were still enthusiastic: The judge's refusal to allow testimony about Natalie's parents' nonchalance at the hospital was plain error. Of course the judge had denied Audrey's motion for a new trial: He wasn't going to admit making a mistake. But surely the appellate court would see it differently.

...

August 2000—two years, one month later. It had taken more than eighteen months for a decision on the appeal: denied. The lawyers had immediately filed another appeal, to the Wisconsin Supreme Court. That decision came unusually fast: in two months the court refused even to consider it.

So the lawyers were now trying something different: They were filing a habeas corpus action—essentially appealing to a federal court. Again the lawyers were hopeful: The trial judge's refusal to allow Audrey to introduce evidence of the parents' behavior at the hospital was unconstitutional. The constitutionality of the judge's ruling was an issue the Wisconsin appellate courts hadn't considered, but the federal court now would.

Meanwhile, Audrey's good behavior for the past three and a half years had earned her one small improvement: She'd been moved from maximum to medium security, living in an open dorm with sixty others, like a large army barracks. *Open space!* Finally, she'd escaped perpetual lockup in a closet. And she could take showers and use the phones and do her laundry and walk the grounds outdoors (9 a.m.–6 p.m.). It was calmer in the dorm: Nobody had to shout. There were more windows.

As much as medium beat maximum, however, it housed many disturbed people, some pathological. Audrey had a locker for her personal belongings that she padlocked. Still, some of the inmates could jimmy the lock in no time. Audrey would return from the gym or a visit to find it missing, her locker door hanging open, and her belongings gone.

The lock did not necessarily disappear forever. Arguments among the inmates could get violent quickly, and some inmates would drop padlocks into socks—"lock in a sock," they called it—and bash each other with the improvised slings. Nor was violence limited to the dorm; a disagreement in the dining room once erupted into a bloody brawl among a dozen inmates.

Another problem was snitches. Some prisoners who'd overheard confessions or the scheming conversations of others would demand favors in return for not reporting to the authorities. Other times, prisoners would invent statements, including confessions, and tell prison staff in order to gain benefits for themselves.

Audrey managed to avoid the violence, intrigue and deceit by keeping to herself. Her isolation was a survival technique. In prison, measuring the positives really meant excluding negatives—that is, skirting the thugs and liars.

But she couldn't avoid the fact that she still faced almost nine more years until her release date. Nine years of concertina wire and concrete and pea-green uniforms and guards, and no kisses and hugs from Dave after work, no children's bedtime stories, no boating on the lake, painting the fence, picking up the dry cleaning, enjoying a glass of wine, weeding the garden, ordering out for pizza, or deciding whether the county road would be quicker than the interstate. Life in confinement was a tablespoon of life.

...

January 2003—two years, five months later. Audrey's attorneys had filed the habeas corpus action: hope restored. Now, after two years—half a college career—it was rejected: despair. But they were appealing the decision: hope revived.

Meanwhile, Audrey had achieved an additional prisoner's perk: Her prison job entitled her to a semiprivate room—room, not cell; living space, not cage. She and her roommate could lock and unlock the room's deadbolt themselves. No more vulnerable padlocks. They even had a curtain around the toilet.

But then Dave, the man she loved, the father of her children, wanted to quit ferrying the kids to and from the prison. He was filing for divorce. He said he'd lost hope after her first parole hearing—four and a half years into her sentence—and now, after six years, he had no idea how much longer he would have to keep up the week-end round trips, or maintain a household for her. Audrey wept, heartbroken, but there was no way she could stop it. Marriage counseling, for example, was no option. Moreover, Dave had a ready-made argument in favor of full custody of the children: Audrey was a convicted, unrepentant child murderer.

Dave wanted exclusive parental rights: no longer would he have to bring the kids to the prison, or pay for the gas (and motel when they stayed the night), or foot the two-hundred-dollar-per-month bill for Audrey's collect calls home.

Abandoned by the one adult on whose love and support she'd counted, Audrey fought not to lose the children, too. She burned through seven thousand dollars of the savings she'd accumulated, before entering prison, by retaining a lawyer. A year passed. The divorce was awarded, but Audrey won a critical victory: Although the court granted Dave a divorce and principal custody, Audrey retained her parental rights, and Dave was ordered to bring the children to her once a month and more often during their vacations. In addition, she was entitled to call the children four times a week at Dave's home. Because these had to be collect calls, they'd get charged to Dave, but the court ordered Audrey to reimburse him twenty-five dollars per month—not easy on her microscopic income. As anguished as she was about the divorce, Audrey was relieved the outcome wasn't worse.

And then, more despair: The appeal of the habeas corpus decision was dismissed. The court ruled that no constitutional violations had occurred during her trial.

Now there were no more courts to turn to. Halfway through her sentence, Audrey faced six more years in the Wisconsin prison system, her children growing up without her, no husband's love to turn to. Her legal and emotional desolation resembled the aftermath of war.

...

June 2003—five months later. Hope for Audrey reappeared, and by chance. A physician who knew about her conviction happened to meet a principal of the Wisconsin Innocence Project. This physician also knew that shaken baby syndrome was now considered unreliable by many medical experts. Convinced by the physician's arguments, the Wisconsin Innocence Project soon took up her case. The Project's faculty and students were enthusiastic, and buoyed her.

Still, Audrey faced the glacial pace of litigation. The Wisconsin Innocence Project was fueled by the effort of law students, whose attention to Audrey's case during the school year was interrupted by their summer vacations and graduation. Then those students' replacements had to study Audrey's voluminous files all over again. As Audrey understood by now, compared with other forms of combat, the law knows little emergency.

...

JOHN C. BURKE CORRECTIONAL CENTER
WAUPUN, WISCONSIN

December 2004—one year, six months later. Audrey had been a paradigm of a prisoner—cooperative and productive—for the nearly eight years she'd been in custody. That behavior earned her a transfer out of Taycheedah to the John C. Burke minimum security facility. There she was entitled to a private room, and a job off prison grounds; she worked at a recycling center, sorting used metal truck and tractor parts for nine dollars an hour.

This filthy job befitted her emotionally filthy circumstances. Her room may have been private, but she couldn't hang a picture on a wall, or have a plant, or put curtains in her window. Her toilet was still metal. Her mattress was still thin, vinyl-covered foam. Her pillow still felt and sounded "like a bag of potato chips." She had to pay the prison twenty dollars per day "rent" for her private room. And she was looking at four more years, without her children.

Two months after she moved into Burke, she attended her second parole hearing. It was mandatory, and it was perfunctory: Audrey wouldn't admit the crime, so she hadn't been "rehabilitated." No parole, and no further parole hearing for thirty months. And although the students and faculty of the Wisconsin Innocence Project were still encouraging, it had been one and a half years since the Project had taken the case, and no legal action had begun. Time dribbled by.

...

June 2006—one year, six months later. The Wisconsin Innocence Project filed a motion for a new trial, based on the revised, negative appraisal of shaken baby syndrome. In fact, now—nine and a half years after Audrey's conviction—the physician who'd served as the prosecution's principal expert witness against Audrey stated that he regretted his earlier testimony and was prepared to retract it.

While this was good news for Audrey, it came with a reservation: the judge who would consider the motion was the same one who'd presided over Audrey's trial.

This time the judge took only six months to deny it. Nevertheless, Audrey was encouraged by reassurances from her supporters that the judge was wrong. If ever there was a reason for a new trial, this was it, and the appeal they'd just filed had a good chance.

...

August 2007—one year, two months later. In her pea-green uniform, Audrey continues across the visiting area on her way to the parole hearing, nodding hello to Sally, the heroin-addicted woman who prefers being in prison.

Audrey enters a large hallway, then sits on a wood chair against one wall. After a while a door on the other side of the hall opens, and a woman appears. She's portly, short brown-and-gray hair, wears glasses. Audrey recognizes her: Harriet Smith, the officer who conducted her previous parole hearings.

"Audrey Edmunds?" she asks. She apparently doesn't recognize Audrey, an indication of the size of her caseload and the long intervals between Audrey's parole hearings.

Audrey nods.

The woman beckons her inside.

The room is a little longer than Audrey's old living room in Waunakee. There is no other door. There are no windows. A dry-erase whiteboard hangs on one wall. In the middle of the room is an old wood table, painted white, with two chairs flanking it.

Smith sits in one of them and bows as she studies papers in a file folder open on the table before her. Beside the file is a recording device.

As Audrey approaches, Smith does not look up, but gestures with one hand for her to sit. She reaches with the other to begin the recording.

"Your name for the record."

"Audrey Edmunds."

"Prisoner number."

"327251."

Smith scans the file in front of her.

"On November 26, 1996, you were convicted of the first-degree reckless homicide of an infant." She looks up at Audrey. "You shook her to death."

Audrey stares back at her, clenches her jaw with frustration, but says nothing.

Smith continues reading: "You were sentenced to eighteen years in prison. Since then you filed a motion for a new trial in July 1997, an appeal from the denial of that motion in July 1998, an appeal from the denial of that appeal in July 1999, a lawsuit in federal court in August 2000, an appeal from the denial. . . ." Smith recites every motion, lawsuit and appeal Audrey's lawyers have filed, including the most recent motion for a new trial.

Smith turns to another document in the file. "This is the third hearing concerning your parole. Instead of admitting your guilt, you continue to clog the courts' dockets with motions and appeals."

Audrey remains silent. It takes an effort to subdue her mounting outrage. *Damn right I do.*

"If you'll admit your guilt," the officer continues, "I can give you a shorter deferment to your next parole hearing—four months instead of eleven."

A "shorter deferment" means the next parole hearing occurs more quickly than scheduled. At each of her previous parole hearings, Smith has promised a shorter deferment if Audrey will admit killing the baby. Other than waiting out her prison term, confessing will be the only means to reunite with those who need her most. Is she being selfish by not confessing? The price she will pay is having "child murderer" seared on her forever, poisoning her relationship with everyone, especially her children.

Besides, it's unlikely to shorten her imprisonment. The parole system is a sham. Smith knows, Audrey knows, and each knows the other knows that a "shorter deferment" is a false carrot, attractive only to fools who hope to escape the stick with which confinement whips them daily. Wisconsin's current sentencing system, called "truth in sentencing," has effectively terminated parole. The parole officer is a puppet whose sole job is to dangle that carrot and wield that merciless stick: "You shook her to death."

The savagery of this process is enraging. Audrey stares into the other woman's eyes, scans her face, then back to her eyes, and perceives only power and disdain and boredom.

Audrey pushes her chair away from the table and stands, turns her back on Smith and the deceit and walks out of the room.

In the hall, the demons rise to meet her: Fury comingles with pain, resentment, horror, heartache, despair— her ruthless companions for more than a decade. Her uniform seems to confine her with zip-locked cruelty. The fluorescent lights are freshly harsh. The concrete around her radiates *prison*.

She turns left and reenters the nightmare.

...

Five months after that parole hearing, Audrey learned the Wisconsin Court of Appeals had reversed the trial judge's decision and awarded her a new trial. Because there was now substantial medical doubt about the reliability of shaken baby syndrome, the court said, there was a "reasonable probability" that a retrial would result in Audrey's acquittal. The court reversed the trial judge's decision, calling it an abuse of his discretion. Six days after learning of the decision, Audrey was freed. Some months later, the prosecution dropped the case.

Audrey now lives in a town of about fourteen hundred in Wisconsin. She works in a bistro at a dairy, serving wine for customers who come to sample the dairy's many varieties of cheese.

Reunification with her children was Audrey's dream come true, and to this day the four retain close emotional bonds. The youngest two attend college in Wisconsin, and the oldest lives and works in Cleveland. Audrey has no grandchildren, so far. She has not remarried. A book about her experience, It Happened to Audrey: A Terrifying Journey from Loving Mom to Accused Baby Killer, *cowritten with Jill Wellington, was released in 2012.*

———

GAYLE LYNDS is hailed as the queen of espionage thrillers. She is the two-time winner of the Military Writers Society of America's award for best novel, and her work has been nominated for numerous other awards. She is married to **JOHN SHELDON**, a retired prosecutor, defense attorney, judge and former visiting scholar to Harvard Law School. Frequent cowriters, John and Gayle live happily in Maine, far from the urban jungles about which they write.

Editors' Note:

In 1971, Dr. A. Norman Guthkelch observed that the shaking of babies could result in "whiplash," subdural hematoma, retinal bleeding and other symptoms, even though there was no external evidence of head injury to the babies. Such injuries often lead to severe disability or death. "Shaken baby syndrome," as Guthkelch's diagnosis was later named, became the basis for numerous prosecutions of caregivers—almost wholly women.

On January 31, 2008, the Wisconsin Court of Appeals granted Audrey Edmunds a new trial based on "competing credible medical opinions in determining whether there is a reasonable doubt as to Edmunds's guilt." Specifically, the appeals court found that "Edmunds presented evidence that was not discovered until after her conviction, in the form of expert medical testimony, that a significant and legitimate debate in the medical community has developed in the past ten years over whether infants can be fatally injured through shaking alone, whether an infant may suffer head trauma and yet experience a significant lucid interval prior to death, and whether other causes may mimic the symptoms traditionally viewed as indicating shaken baby or shaken impact syndrome."[1]

The controversy continues. Dr. Guthkelch has stepped

---

1   *State of Wisconsin v. Audrey A. Edmunds, Wisconsin Court Opinions* (January 31, 2008).

back from his position that the symptoms are always indic-
ative of criminal conduct, expressing disappointment in
the way his diagnosis has been appropriated by using
the science as a way to convict people.[2] Meanwhile, the
National Center for the Review and Prevention of Child
Deaths in the United States continues to argue for study,
worried that as a result of the current scientific confusion,
guilty child abusers are going unpunished.

---

2   "The Anatomy of a Murder Case," by RetroREPORT,
    New York Times, September 13, 2015, http://www.nytimes
    .com/video/us/100000003906982/retro-report-voices-
    the-lawyer.html?playlistId=1194811622182.

Alton Logan with Laura Caldwell, left. Photo courtesy of Life After Innocence

8.

THE WRONG MAN

THE CRUELTIES OF FATE

Alton Logan (Illinois exoneree),
as told to **Jan Burke**

———

BAD THINGS HAPPEN to good people. Those who are charged with protecting and serving the people sometimes become blind to the immorality of the methods they use to achieve what they firmly believe are lofty objectives; sometimes, as the saying goes, absolute power simply corrupts absolutely. Sometimes the very rules of law that are designed to ensure the best defense for one man can work to punish another. Alton Logan suffered for twenty-six years because of such rules.

For those who grew up, as Alton Logan did, in the 1960s, Richard Speck was the monster of their childhood.

Few who were children then could fail to remember the shocking news stories about the mass murderer.

No one could have foreseen how profoundly Speck's later actions would affect the life of Alton Logan, wrongfully imprisoned in Illinois. Monster that he was, Speck reached out from the grave.

...

Born in rural Illinois in 1941, Richard Speck was six when his father died. His destitute mother then married a man who had a criminal past and drank heavily, and who moved his wife and stepson to Dallas, Texas. Speck hated him.

By the time he was fifteen, Speck was an alcoholic and drug addict, and soon became a petty criminal. He dropped out of high school. His criminal activities only increased over time, including spousal abuse, aggravated assault, forgery, burglary, robbery and more. Somewhere along the way he had his wrist tattooed with the words, "Born to Raise Hell." Following a divorce, and with a warrant out for his arrest for robbing a grocery store, he fled back to Illinois, where his older siblings still lived.

Although initially seeking a fresh start, Speck soon engaged in even more violent crimes than those he had committed in Texas. In his hometown, he raped a sixty-five-year-old woman at knifepoint. He was suspected in the small town, brought in for questioning by police and soon took off for Chicago, where one of his married sisters lived.

After a brief stint in the Merchant Marines, he drifted through Chicago again, where on July 13, 1966, he took

THE WRONG MAN: THE CRUELTIES OF FATE

a room at the Shipyard Inn. He followed a woman from bar to bar through the day, then that evening forced her at knifepoint to his room, where he raped her. He stole her .22 pistol from her purse, then made his way to a townhouse that housed a community of student nurses. He knocked on the door, and when it was opened by Corazon Amurao, leveled his gun at her face and forced his way in. He rounded up the young women who were home, tied them up and proceeded to rape, torture and murder them one by one. Those women who had been out for the evening and arrived later were also attacked. Over those horrific hours, he robbed, raped, beat, strangled and stabbed eight women between the ages of nineteen and twenty-four.

There were nine women in the building. One survived.

In his frenzy, Speck had lost track of the first woman he had confronted. Corazon Amurao had managed to hide herself under a bed. She cowered there for hours, finally emerging on a balcony where she screamed for help. By then, Speck was on the run.

The news of the killings made headlines and broadcasts around the world. Amurao's description, particularly of his "Born to Raise Hell" tattoo, and the intensive media attention on the case led to his arrest six days later. Speck had tried to commit suicide, then faltered and called for help. A doctor at the hospital saw the tattoo on Speck's injured wrist and notified police.

Speck was convicted in April 1967 and sentenced to death. In 1972, the U.S. Supreme Court abolished capital punishment (although leaving the door open for its reinstatement in future cases) and Speck's sentence was commuted: fifty to one hundred years in prison. As Alton Logan said many years later, "Speck was a man who knew that he would never see the outside of the institution."

...

On the evening of January 11, 1982, Lloyd Wickliffe was working as a security guard in a McDonald's on Halsted Street on Chicago's far South Side. At a little past eight, during an armed robbery attempt, Wickliffe was killed by a shotgun blast, and another security guard, Alvin Thompson, was wounded. The attackers, Edgar Hope and Andrew Wilson, did not get any money, but they stole the handguns the guards were carrying.

Alton Logan was home asleep, nowhere near the robbery.

Later the wounded guard, Thompson, was questioned and correctly identified Edgar Hope as one of the shooters. Thompson misidentified the second shooter as Alton Logan. The police found two other witnesses to say the same.

...

On February 5, Edgar Hope was arrested after he shot and killed a police officer on a Chicago Transit Authority bus, and wounded a second officer. The gun he used to shoot the officers was the weapon stolen from Thompson.

Meanwhile, based on Thompson's mistaken identification, Alton Logan was arrested. "I thought they were crazy," Alton said. His mother and brother both said he had been at home the night of the robbery, but police ignored them.

On February 9, two days after Alton was charged, two Chicago police officers, William Fahey and Richard O'Brien, were shot to death. As with the McDonald's guards, the officers' guns were taken.

Mayor Jane Byrne and police superintendent Richard Brzeczek responded with a widespread search for the killers, soon suspected to be Andrew Wilson and his brother, Jackie. It would be the most intense manhunt in the city's history, marked by brutality and the abuse of many innocent African American citizens. Over two hundred complaints were filed, although the department would claim it lost many of them.

The detective placed in charge of that search was Jon Burge, recently promoted to lieutenant and head of the department's new Area Two Violent Crimes Unit.

On February 13, that search led police to raid a beauty parlor where they believed Andrew Wilson had been hiding. Wilson wasn't there, but they found the guns that had been stolen from Officer Fahey and Officer O'Brien. They also found a shotgun. Crime lab tests would show it had been used in the McDonald's shooting.

Instead of releasing Alton Logan, who continued to tell them that he had not been Hope's partner in the robbery, they ignored this physical evidence.

No physical evidence would ever link Alton Logan to the McDonald's case.

When the Wilson brothers were arrested on February 14, Chicago police found a .38 in Andrew's possession. It was a stolen handgun—taken from Lloyd Wickliffe, the McDonald's guard killed by Wilson. Police not only didn't release Alton, they hid this evidence from prosecutors.

Andrew Wilson was taken by Burge, who already had a long history of torturing arrestees, to a place where Burge and one of his detectives subjected Wilson to electric shocks from a hand-cranked generator—Burge referred to it as his "nigger box"—on the nose, ears, lips and genitals. They placed plastic bags over his head and nearly suffocated him. They beat him. They burned him with a cigarette lighter. They handcuffed him across a hot, ribbed steam radiator and administered shocks that caused him to jolt against it.

The injuries were so bad, the police lockup refused to accept him. By the end of the day of his arrest, he was in Mercy Hospital. His injuries were documented by his attorney's investigators and by medical personnel. Dr. John Raba, who examined Wilson, wrote to police superintendent Richard Brzeczek, demanding an investigation. Brzeczek forwarded the letter to State's Attorney Richard M. Daley, but Daley declined to investigate.

...

About a month after Wilson's arrest, Edgar Hope told his attorney that Alton had not been the other shooter, that it was Wilson who had been with him that night. Several eyewitnesses said the same, some identifying Wilson as the shooter.

Edgar Hope's attorney, Marc Miller, went to one of Andrew Wilson's attorneys, Jamie Kunz, and told him what Hope had said about their client. Kunz and Dale Coventry were Wilson's court-appointed Cook County assistant public defenders. They then approached Wilson and asked if it was true that he had been with Hope that night and killed Wickliffe.

Wilson chuckled and acknowledged that Hope was telling the truth. "That was me." He was gleeful, looking pleased at letting an innocent man pay for his crime.

The attorneys were bound by attorney-client privilege— one of the most basic and revered legal concepts. It ensures that communications between an attorney and his or her client are confidential, and that a client need not worry that the attorney will be forced to reveal those communications. It is a privilege that courts have supported since the sixteenth century. Wilson knew his attorneys were ethically and legally bound never to divulge any part of any conversation he held with them, and he refused to give them permission to disclose what he had told them. Without permission of the client, this privilege extends even after the death of the client. Eventually, Wilson agreed to sign an affidavit stating that he was the one who had been with Edgar Hope that night and that he was guilty of killing Wickliffe—on the condition that it could not be revealed until after his death.

...

Alton Logan now found himself in an almost unimaginable situation. No one would listen to his protestations of innocence. He knew the truth, but to a set of people within the Chicago Police Department and the state's attorney's office, winning convictions was more important than the truth. Because they had allegations filed against two shooters, they weren't going to take a second look.

Evidence was withheld. Individuals were coerced into giving rehearsed testimony, and Alton Logan was found guilty.

Attorney Dale Coventry attended Alton's sentencing, his stomach in knots at the thought that the jury might give an innocent man the death penalty, knowing of the existence of a piece of paper that could spare him. If Alton was given the death sentence, Coventry could save his life, because under those circumstances, the canons of ethics would allow him to come forward with his information.

"The vote was 10–2," Alton said. "Ten for, two against. Two individuals saved my life." But those same two individuals unknowingly condemned Alton to years of unjustified punishment.

The attorneys remained constrained by attorney-client privilege to keep silent. The affidavit went into a lockbox under Dale Coventry's bed.

...

Alton Logan said to himself, "You have to mentally adjust. You do not know what to expect. You do not know the situation. Your mind has to focus on one thing and one thing only: survival."

Survival meant understanding that you would be "living your life under the control of somebody else. The only control you have is over your own mind."

It was an important realization. A year later, another man who had entered prison at the same time as Alton was "heavily medicated. He was just a shell of himself."

Alton Logan had something else driving his desire to survive. "From day one, I knew I didn't do it. That was all I was concerned with. To rectify it."

So he learned how to dig down deep into himself to find that control over his own mind, and how to dig down deep into his own case.

He spent the first fourteen years of his imprisonment in Pontiac Correctional Institution. Pontiac, the oldest prison in Illinois, was built in 1871, over one hundred years before Alton was sent there. At the time, Illinois prison populations were 50 percent or more above the number they were designed to hold. Pontiac was no exception. Its three cell houses were crowded.

Cells designed to hold two inmates were eight feet long, ten feet wide, eight feet high, but sometimes two inmates were placed in cells only eight by five by eight. Each row of cells faced a cell house wall that had one window. In one corner of the cell, open to the view of anyone in the cell or looking into it, was a metal unit with a sink above a metal toilet. Each cell had a steel dresser. The noise created by the activities of inmates and guards was constant. Ventilation was poor, and the buildings were hot in the summer and cold in winter. Roaches and mice were everywhere.

Separated from his family and friends, a future of an unknown number of years of incarceration lying before him, choices most enjoy without thinking were taken from him. No deciding what time he would rise, eat or sleep. No choosing what he would eat. No choosing who would be in the small cell with him.

Some of the cell mates were easier to get along with than others. "I had my share of bad cellies," he said.

And yet there were ways people showed respect for one another, both guards and cell mates. "You would put a sheet up in front of the toilet when one of you had to use it. That was something private. The guards respected that."

Like most inmates, Alton concealed a handmade weapon in his cell for self-defense. Three times shakedowns led to his being segregated on weapons charges. Segregation meant that he was isolated twenty-four hours a day. "In segregation, you are only allowed to be outside by yourself once a week to take a shower, and once a week to go out into the yard." He survived a year of segregation.

Once in the courtroom he "cussed out the judge and the attorneys," telling them, "there's nothing you can do to me. What can you do to hurt me?"

As his first decade in prison passed, he set his mind not only to survive but to preserve his sense of self, his self-control. "You know how it works. You just have to dig down deep into yourself. You stay out of nonsense. Try not to get into trouble."

He did what he could for himself. By 1996, his daily routine was to wake at 8:30 a.m., then go to work at whatever job the prison would give him, attend school (which was then still offered by Illinois institutions), or jog around and around and around the yard. Then he spent time in the prison law library, working on his case. His day would typically end at about 9 p.m.

He learned that with the small amount of money his family would give to his account, he could purchase food from the commissary to supplement what was served in the cafeteria. He might be able to buy little things to help pass the time—a deck of cards, a component set to listen to music, a small television set. Jeans were sold in the commissary. He could paint the walls of his cell.

All of that would change overnight.

One morning in 1996, Alton Logan woke to discover that the entire prison was on lockdown. "Word came up.

I couldn't believe it, and all because of Speck." Richard Speck was in the news again, four years after his death.

...

In May 1996, Bill Kurtis, an investigative journalist and former CBS anchor, received a disturbing videotape. Within weeks, Kurtis showed it publicly to the members of the Illinois state legislature, who had packed the chambers to view it. The video, two hours long, had been made by an unknown person, taped inside Stateville prison. It showed Richard Speck snorting what appeared to be cocaine, flashing cash, bragging about the comforts of his life in prison.

Speck's appearance was startlingly changed: At the bidding of an unknown male with him, he removed most of his clothing to reveal feminine underwear, then went on to show that he now had enlarged, drooping breasts. Speck talked of obtaining illicit hormone injections while in prison.

He casually discussed murdering his victims, describing the killings in callous detail and bragging about his strength in overpowering and strangling them. Asked by another inmate why he had killed them, he laughed and mockingly said, "It just wasn't their night." He admitted to having no feelings about the murders, and said, "If you're asking me if I felt sorry, no."

He crowed about his comforts in prison, and tauntingly said, "If they knew how much fun I was having in here, they'd turn me loose." When he began performing oral sex on another inmate, the outraged legislators halted the showing of the tape.

...

No one at Pontiac prison knew the tape would be shown on television. But when it came on, word spread like wildfire through the prison. The cell blocks grew quiet.

...

The next morning was when Alton woke up to discover the entire prison was on lockdown.

"We were in trouble," Alton said. "I deduced what had happened. The government had no idea what was going on inside the prison system. They wanted to take the institutions back."

What Alton and others inside knew was that drugs were routinely available in the prisons, that in fact gangs were running the prisons. Now the legislature knew that, too.

"They appointed a special committee to investigate. They locked down every institution in the state."

Guards began going through the prison cell by cell on a search-and-destroy mission, confiscating not only contraband, but also materials that previously were permitted, items that had been sold to prisoners from the prison commissary. No more food, no more jeans. "We were given about two to three hours to turn up our cells and send home anything not allowed."

Small things that made life in prison a little more bearable disappeared.

The rules he had lived with for over a decade changed in an instant.

...

For months, the prisoners were confined to their cells with no communication with the outside world. No visitors. Those small, windowless cells designed to hold a single inmate became the only world inmates knew.

Instead of the chow hall, the guards brought the meals on trays that were pushed through a slot. No more commissary food—these meals just passed the standard of "edible." For prisoners who were diabetic, as many were, there was an additional problem—there was no choice but to eat the high-starch foods served three times a day.

"You learned that you had to make readjustments."

Those readjustments meant that for two months, Alton and his cellie played cards, watched TV, read books, played chess. "Although cellies might aggravate each other at times, you learned to use your head and not your emotions." He lost his ability to attend school, to work.

Prisoners communicated using hand mirrors and by "screaming and hollering up and down the gallery."

After a month, prisoners were allowed a couple of hours in the yard, one gallery at a time. Later, these small groups were allowed to eat in the chow hall together.

Searches were a constant.

"Some guards changed. The ones we were able to be human with, who showed some compassion, didn't change. The assholes got worse."

Guards got in trouble, too, as corruption was exposed.

In 1997, Pontiac became all-segregation, all the time. Inmates would spend all but one or two hours a day in cells by themselves. Many inmates were sent to other facilities, often to Menard, another maximum security prison. Alton talked to the assistant warden, asking to be sent to Stateville. Only forty miles from Chicago, Stateville could be reached by those who would make the five visits allowed each month. But if visitors wanted to see a prisoner in Menard, they had to travel to southern Illinois, an eight-hour drive, and rent a hotel room. Visits would be expensive and time-consuming, and necessarily become less frequent.

Alton went to Stateville.

Stateville prison was built in 1925 on the "panopticon" model, commonly known as a roundhouse. In the roundhouses, four floors of jail cells form a circle around a central armed tower that sits inside a large, open concrete floor. The prisoners can be watched at all times from the tower. If needed, they can be shot from the guns stationed there. Sound constantly bounces off the hard surfaces of walls, floors and ceiling.

It was an environment entirely different from that of

Pontiac, with only one thing in common: overcrowding. Although the design was less confined than at Pontiac, no cell was out of the sight of guards and others.

Much changed for prisoners in Illinois over the next two years, as it did everywhere in the country. Federal funding for the education of prisoners was cut, and the program that had once allowed Alton to obtain a degree was shut down.

The quality of the food continued to decline. It was cheaper to feed inmates food made from soybeans rather than meat.

Alton continued to make use of the prison library. He maintained hope. Someday, someone would come forward and tell the truth. He learned more about cases that had a connection to his own: Detective Jon Burge.

More light was being shed on the brutal and unjust activities of Burge and his crew. In 1994, Burge was fired from the Chicago Police Department. As more torture cases came to public attention, the state at last began to respond to criticism and allegations from local and international human rights groups.

In 2000, concerned by these reports, Illinois governor George Ryan declared a moratorium on the death penalty. In 2002, a special prosecutor was appointed to look into the allegations of torture. In 2003, Ryan said, "Because our three-year study has found only more questions about the fairness of the sentencing; because of the spectacular failure to reform the system; because we have seen justice delayed for countless death row inmates with potentially meritorious claims; because the Illinois death penalty system is arbitrary and capricious—and therefore immoral—I no longer shall tinker with the machinery of death. . . . Because of all of these reasons today I am commuting the sentences of all death row inmates. This is a blanket commutation." Four death row inmates received pardons.

The findings of the special prosecutor were that although many of the allegations against Burge were true, the statute of limitations had been exceeded in almost all cases, and civil claims and criminal charges against Burge and the City would be barred. Richard M. Daley, who was by then Chicago's mayor, and other authorities were excluded from the report.

...

On November 19, 2007, Andrew Wilson, the man who had committed the murder and attempted murder for which Alton was convicted, died in prison of natural causes. Attorneys Kunz and Coventry were free to present their affidavit to the court showing, in effect, that an innocent man was in prison. They did so in January 2008.

Four months later, on April 18, 2008, Alton Logan was released on bond. He had to wait until September of that year to hear that his case was dismissed. He had survived twenty-six years in prison. During that time, his mother, who believed in his innocence and maintained hope for his freedom, had passed away, but his two brothers rejoiced in his release.

Almost a year to the day after his release, on April 17, 2009, Alton was officially declared innocent through a Certificate of Innocence presented by Judge Paul Biebel Jr.

In October 2008, federal prosecutors arrested Jon Burge and charged him with two counts of obstruction of justice and one count of perjury. He was convicted on all counts. He was sentenced to four and a half years, of which he served not quite four years. Groups still fighting for his victims alleged that over twenty African American men remain in prison as a result of confessions coerced by Burge and his associates. Court costs, investigations and lawsuits in connection with Burge's activities have cost the city of Chicago over $100 million.

Alton Logan sued the City, not claiming that he had been tortured, but that Burge and his detectives allegedly hid exculpatory evidence from prosecutors. The City settled in early 2013, allowing Alton to stop relying solely on his family for financial support. Alton still lives in Chicago. He travels often to speak on behalf of those who have been wrongly convicted. "It's not just about me," he says. "There are still other innocent people in there."

JAN BURKE is an Edgar® Award–winning author of numerous mysteries and thrillers and is the founder of the Crime Lab Project, an organization devoted to educating legislatures and the public to the problems facing forensic science, including the desperate need for improved training, research and facilities.

Editors' Note

Official misconduct (including arresting officers, detectives and prosecutors) is an element in nearly half of all cases tabulated in the National Registry of Exonerations. The Innocence Project cites the following kinds of misconduct by policing officials: employing suggestion when conducting identification procedures, coercing false confessions, failing to turn over exculpatory evidence to the prosecution and providing incentives to secure unreliable evidence from informants. Common forms of misconduct by prosecutors include withholding exculpatory evidence from the defense; deliberately mishandling, mistreating or destroying evidence; allowing witnesses they know or should know are not truthful to testify; pressuring defense witnesses not to testify; relying on known fraudulent forensic experts; and making misleading arguments that overstate the probative value of testimony.

Peter Reilly

9.

LUCK AND THE DEATH PENALTY

COMMUNITY INVOLVEMENT

An essay about **Peter Reilly**
(Connecticut exoneree)
by **Arthur Miller**

———

SOMETIMES NO ONE *in the legal system, nor the
exonerees or their families, can get them out. Sometimes,
the community must rally around them. The release of
the West Memphis Three (three teenagers wrongfully
convicted of an allegedly satanic murder) was widely credited to the community at large and the efforts of celebrities like Johnny Depp, Patti Smith and Eddie Vedder.
The following essay by the renowned playwright Arthur
Miller is published here for the first time with the kind
permission of the Arthur Miller Estate. Peter Reilly, the
subject of the following essay, was accused of murdering
his mother. On September 29, 1973, Peter, then eighteen, allegedly told the State Police during an eight-hour*

*interrogation, "I definitely did what happened to my
mother last night." He confessed to battering, stomping
on, repeatedly stabbing, raping and nearly decapitating
the only parent he ever knew, Barbara Gibbons, fifty-one.
On the basis of his confession, he was convicted.*

It is a small town so everybody knew the boy. He was
approaching eighteen but he was slight, blond and
soft-spoken so he was referred to as a boy. His mildness
made it hard for many to believe that he had butchered
his mother even after the State Police announced that he
had made a confession. In fact, the longer his trial went
on, the fewer the folks who felt convinced of his guilt.

Still, strange things do happen and he was convicted and was actually in a car on his way to the State
Penitentiary when a group of residents raised enough
money—some even mortgaging their homes—to lodge
an appeal, and he was returned to the local jail. Basically
a conservative community, many people there had rather
unwillingly come to believe that the confession had
somehow been forced out of him by the police.

At the hearing to decide whether to give him a new
trial, things did not look good; the second judge seemed
a fair and sympathetic listener but the defense, now under
a new lawyer, was required to produce new evidence,
not easy to get hold of. But several days into the hearing the state's attorney who had gotten the boy convicted
dropped dead on a golf course and a substitute prosecutor

immediately took his place and began studying his papers on the case.

In the files the substitute discovered an affidavit from a witness who swore that he and his wife had seen the boy in another part of town at the very moment his mother was being attacked and killed. This affidavit had been withheld from evidence, never introduced into the original trial despite the witness being a policeman who had known the boy and had not the slightest doubt that he had recognized him. Introduced into the hearing the very next morning, the affidavit blew the state's case out of the water and the boy was freed.

If the state of Connecticut had had a death penalty, the boy may well have been executed. The boy's mother had been nearly eviscerated, savagely mauled, and feelings of disgust and anger were aroused. Indeed, it was only the adventitious death of the prosecutor that saved the boy from a long sentence in a penitentiary that would probably have destroyed him, gentle and mild as he was. Connecticut is not normally considered a benighted state but one with a very high income level, and a large proportion of educated people. Yet this travesty happened there.

Any honest supporter of the death penalty simply cannot avoid facing the high probability of mistaken verdicts, of which there are indeed many in this country. The nation's conscience forbids the state to kill innocent people. The death penalty makes the presumption that there are never going to be corrupt, ambitious, cowardly prosecutors and police who, afraid to admit they were wrong in arresting a suspect, go down to the end insisting on his guilt; that there are never honest mistakes in judgment, never any visual misidentifications, but that in each and every prosecution the guilty verdict is invariably deserved.

The boy, Peter Reilly, regained his freedom in Litchfield County because a prosecutor died at the propitious time and because his neighbors believed in him, and outsiders were moved to come to his aid. The life of the innocent cannot be allowed to depend on that much luck nor the states dishonored by pretensions of infallibility in absolutely every capital case that comes before its all but overwhelmed courts.

For three years, much of the community was up in arms about the Peter Reilly conviction. To his friends and neighbors, his innocence was obvious. They could not understand how a dubious confession, reportedly obtained by high-pressure psychological persuasion, could be credited in the absence of any corroborating evidence. The medical findings suggested at least two attackers. Furthermore, Peter had no known motive to kill his mother.

Reporter Donald S. Connery, writing for the Hartford Courant in 2013, recounts the story: "Bake sales and other efforts raised $60,000 to free Peter on bond for the appeal. The convicted killer was welcomed back *at his high school to complete his senior year. Roxbury playwright Arthur Miller organized a powerful rescue party—a new attorney, a crack investigator, the nation's leading forensic pathologist and a top expert on mind control. Superb reporting by the* Hartford Courant's *Joseph A. O'Brien and critical editorials in the* Lakeville Journal *raised alarming questions about the State Police investigation. The case became a national sensation.*

"After a long hearing for a new trial in 1976, Superior Court Judge John A. Speziale, the future state chief justice, declared that a 'grave injustice' occurred in his courtroom two years earlier."

After deciding to proceed with a retrial, State's Attorney John Bianchi dropped dead on a golf course. His successor, Dennis Santore, however, discovered a time bomb: a critical document, never revealed to the defense or the court. The document revealed the testimony of an auxiliary state trooper and his wife, placing Peter five miles away at the time the state claimed he was home killing his mother. The retrial never occurred.

———

ARTHUR MILLER sent this essay in 2002 to Rob Warden, executive director of the Center on Wrongful Convictions at Northwestern University's School of Law, to be used in a campaign to eliminate the death penalty in Illinois. Miller was a longtime opponent of the death penalty. In 1992, he wrote a satirical essay for the *New*

York Times, urging the "privatization" of executions so that they could be used as entertainment events.

Miller's part in the Peter Reilly case was not unprecedented: As long ago as 1907, Sir Arthur Conan Doyle successfully took up the case of a young solicitor imprisoned for a series of cattle mutilations, and eventually wrote a book condemning the police misconduct that led to George Edalji's wrongful conviction. (The events were novelized by Julian Barnes as *Arthur and George* [2005] and recently dramatized.) Although ten thousand people had signed a petition urging Edalji's release, it was Doyle's involvement that brought about the ultimate exoneration.

Editors' Note

Another prominent case that was resolved in significant part because of community pressure was that of the so-called West Memphis Three. Three teenagers who, in 1994, were tried and convicted of the murders of three boys in West Memphis, Arkansas, with much emphasis put on the defendants' wearing of black and listening to Black Sabbath music. The investigation of the crime and the conduct of the trial were criticized extensively in two documentaries, and celebrities including Johnny Depp, Patti Smith and Eddie Vedder took up the cause. After numerous appeals, on August 19, 2011, the defendants were released from prison as part of a plea deal. To the disappointment of many of the West Memphis

Three supporters, the three entered into what are known as "Alford" plea deals,[1] a legal agreement that allows defendants to plead guilty while still asserting their actual innocence, and at the same time admitting the prosecution has evidence against you beyond a reasonable doubt. As a result, the judge sentenced them to "time served," allowing them to be freed but not exonerated. They are still considered, in the eyes of the law, ex-offenders.

---

1 *North Carolina v. Alford*, 400 U.S. 25 (1970).

Ginny Lefever

10.

STAYING ON TRACK

SURVIVING INCARCERATION

Ginny Lefever (Ohio exoneree),
as told to **Sarah Weinman**

———

ONCE INCARCERATED, THE *most difficult tasks for most exonerees—in addition to survival—are to keep hold of their intellectual and spiritual faculties and stay focused on their innocence and the possibility of exoneration. Too often, the mere fact of imprisonment is overwhelming. Most people are ill equipped to cope with the overbearing presence and sometimes sadism of the corrections officers, the mental instability of other prisoners and the sense of isolation and despair brought on by imprisonment. The following is the story of one woman's battle with herself.*

Ginny Lefever didn't wake up one morning and discover she had put on half a person in weight overnight.

It happened, like bankruptcy, slowly, slowly, then all at once, the realization that at 273 pounds, she'd reached her heaviest and could not afford to add pounds to her five-foot-five-inch frame.

Nor could Ginny, in the summer of 1994, afford to give in to the shadow of madness lurking about the prison at the Ohio Reformatory for Women in Marysville. Most days she could remind herself this circumscribed, ritual-bound life was real. That she was serving a life sentence for the murder of her husband, a murder she did not commit. Most days Ginny could carry on the fight, enlisting lawyers to appeal on her behalf, bucking up at every denial, every upheld judgment, every bit of bad news.

But then there were times she turned on the television and felt like the news belonged to another planet. There were more than a few moments when Ginny felt the prison walls move in tighter around her body and mind. She couldn't see out. She couldn't see streets or cars. She could hardly hear noise that wasn't tied to the prison. The rational part of her knew better. But the rational part couldn't battle that lurking shadow forever. Not unless Ginny did something about it. And if she didn't do something now, she feared she never would. Then the shadow would win, taking what remained of her hope.

She'd spent the past four years essentially eating herself to death. She would no more. She'd spent an equal amount of time fighting big battles and losing, fighting little battles and also losing. She could not lose her sanity in the process.

At Marysville, prisoners had access to a circular track. A single lap equaled about a tenth of a mile. On sunny afternoons the track would crowd with other inmates, stupidly grateful for the chance to move around for a short while, happy to get away from regularly scheduled counts, terrible meals and private hells of their own making.

Those other women didn't have Ginny's newfound purpose. She eyed the track as a means to an end. If she walked around, even for a few laps, that shadow might recede. An active body had to help bring her rational mind back to dominance.

She chose a summer day for its dusk delay, for the chance of a few extra hours. Ginny, in orange prison clothes, white off-brand sneakers, a Walkman in her hand attached to the buds in her ears, headed out for the track just after lunch. She took her mark. She got set. She began to walk in a loop.

She barely made it three full times around the track that first day.

Ginny sweated. She waddled. She grunted and groaned. Her legs felt like lead. Her feet ached like she'd walked on molten coal. She was not used to moving so much, even if it was really so little. *Screw this*, Ginny thought, *I don't need to come back tomorrow.*

She came back the next day. She walked around the

full track three times and then some. She went back the day after that. And the day after that. The loops multiplied. The mileage piled up. And so did her resolve: she had to lose the weight, heal her mind, and prove, some way, somehow, she did not kill her husband.

...

As Ginny circled the track, that first time and all those later times, she tried not to dwell on her predicament. But a predicament like hers was hard to ignore. Especially when the fight to save your sense of self was such a lonely fight.

Ginny's sense of self was, before prison, very developed. It had to be. She endured her fair share of strife—hardscrabble origins in rural Ohio. Acting as the mother figure for her younger siblings because her own mother and father had all but checked out of the parenting thing. Getting pregnant at the tail end of high school, marrying the child's father, realizing, as so many in her situation did, that such a marriage was a bad idea. Divorce, then meeting someone new, someone who seemed kind. Someone who listened. Someone who cared. Someone who respected Ginny so she, in turn, could respect herself more.

They married, Ginny and William Lefever, blending their families together, and for a while things were good. Ginny went to nursing school and came close to finishing her bachelor's degree. She worked and looked after the kids, hers and his. And then, gradually at first and suddenly not long after, things went very bad. The birth of a child with severe defects, and his death at the age of nine. Miscarriages. Physical and psychological abuse. Another child's premature passing. And her husband's descent into hard drinking and harder drugs.

By 1988, Ginny's husband was chronically unemployed and chronically addicted. Ginny, thirty-seven at the time, wanted out and prepared to divorce. In August of that year, she received full custody of her children and filed a restraining order against her soon-to-be ex-husband. The Ohio domestic court scheduled a final hearing to grant Ginny her divorce on September 27, 1988.

She never got that hearing.

A week before, on the night of September 20, 1988, William Lefever came back to the house he had once shared with Ginny, to have dinner with the children, per the custody agreement. During the evening Ginny thought William was acting oddly. Her heart sank because that oddness was familiar, so much like the way he behaved while he was on drugs. He wouldn't leave the house after dinner, despite Ginny's insistence that he do so, that the court had ordered him to do so. Instead, William passed out on the couch in the main room.

The next morning William awoke and became belligerent, even combative. Paramedics were called to the house, and they took him to the hospital, where he admitted to taking a bunch of Ginny's antidepressants.

His behavior worsened. His heart gave out. William Lefever, forty-one, died in the hospital.

Despite his words to the doctors, despite Ginny's firm belief her husband was capable of suicide, law enforcement focused on a glaringly obvious needle prick on William's butt. He'd received a deliberate drug overdose, one that did not look self-administered. The cops believed that Ginny did it. The experts—one man in particular—swore Ginny did it with poison. A jury convicted her in February 1990 and sentenced Ginny to life in prison.

And now here she was, hobbling around the track because her life depended on it.

...

Through sweat and tears and grit, Ginny Lefever made it a full mile around the Marysville track. As summer waned and winter dawned, she upped her mileage, day by day, songs like Sting's "If I Ever Lose My Faith in You" the soundtrack to her daily regimen.

The weight dropped off, to the 200 pounds she weighed at trial, to the 170 when she got arrested, and lower and lower. She wasn't anywhere near her high school trim size and maybe never would be. What mattered more was that Ginny kept moving. Pretty soon she got other people's attention. Other women asked to walk with her. "I never intended for that to be a thing," Ginny said, "but it got to be a thing on a small scale."

The other women in prison with her, those who walked with her and even those who did not, thought Ginny had it good in Marysville. She taught a class or two, an hour a week on life and coping strategies. She had her own room when many did not.

She had access to a decent library and read everything she could get her hands on, especially mystery novels by the likes of Grisham, Evanovich and Patterson. It might have been nice to read more women authors. Not romance novels, though. Those would never touch Ginny's hands.

Ginny knew different from what the other prisoners thought about her: She might have looked like she had it good all right, but inside was another matter. Inside her mind, the doubts had room to play. So did the questions about what was real and what was not. The cold spot of anger over her absurd situation. The corrosive belief that hope was a mirage.

The more Ginny walked, the more determined she was to leave Marysville.

That year she walked to save her life, she read through the Bible from start to finish. There was a verse from Deuteronomy that Ginny made her own and kept repeating to herself: "I gotta get off the mountain."

Ginny pleaded her case for a transfer to the warden at the beginning of 2001. It was unusual for a lifer to get approved to be moved to a lower-security prison in Ohio.

But the warden was sympathetic to Ginny and admired her resolve.

"You're crazy," was the general refrain from her fellow inmates. Why would Ginny leave a place where she could be left alone? Where lifers had, however tiny, some measure of personal space, not crowded in like cattle? Going from having your own room to double-bunking with who-knows-what?

But the feeling was that the television channel's broadcast from another galaxy wouldn't leave Ginny be. There was so much she could not control: How the Ohio courts might rule on her latest habeas corpus appeal. Whether someone, anyone, other than the lawyers she paid, would take her insistence of innocence seriously. After each court loss Ginny's determination and desperation increased in tandem.

"My fear was not about whether I would ever get out, but that when I did, there wouldn't be enough left of me to put the pieces back together again," she said. "I knew intellectually and cognitively that I was stuck in some remote hole in central Ohio and that the world outside existed. But my brain would go, 'What if it's something else?'"

It took a few months to process the paperwork for the transfer. Ohio prison bureaucracy does not move quickly. But in July of that year, Ginny got her wish.

Good-bye, Marysville. Hello, Franklin.

...

What hurt Ginny the most was what had happened with her family.

There were four children, theirs and hers, when Ginny was arrested. Her youngest, Alex, was just four years old. Alex went into foster care. Then his foster parents got divorced. Ginny learned that by letter, when it looked like Alex would get sent back into the system.

Ginny and Alex began a phone relationship, which turned into occasional visits when he got older. By then, Alex was almost an adult. He'd been told his mother was an evil monster who murdered his father. The woman sitting across from him did not seem that way at all. She was blunt, yes. Had little patience or soft manner. Prison did that to a woman, sharpened her already serrated edges to Ginsu territory. But slowly Alex began to doubt that she was the coldhearted killer he'd been led to expect. Later, he would have troubles of his own, overcome them and raise a family—Ginny's grandchildren. But for now, though it wasn't much, she was his mother.

Ginny's oldest daughter, Heather, stood by her for her entire prison sentence. Heather wanted to take in the younger kids when Ginny started her sentence. Ginny said no. "You have to live your life," she told Heather, and it was good advice at the time, even though later the distance between them made Ginny sad. Heather, she said, became a different person. It happens. She lived her life, and it took her in a different direction from what Ginny hoped.

The other children said Ginny was guilty from the first and never wavered. Sometimes they said so to the media. Ginny saw the sins of the past repeat again and again. Drinking. Drugs. Custody losses. Peripatetic lives. Ginny blamed it on trauma, unrecognized and untreated.

...

Ginny transferred from Marysville to the Franklin County Corrections Center the week after 9/11. She spent the first week in what's called prerelease, designed to ease the transition from one facility to another. Ginny noticed right away that the place "had a really nice track with a nice view of the highway. I sat on the top bleachers and watched the traffic go by, endlessly. Anytime I didn't have to be somewhere else, I sat and watched the cars go by."

She didn't count them. She didn't do anything more than sit and watch, smell the crisp fall air, hear the engines roar one by one as they whizzed by her down below. But the relief was palpable. Ginny's grip on sanity would stay put. No longer would she feel, as she had in Marysville, that she was stuck in an alternate universe. She could be present. She could find more energy to fight for her release from prison. And she could keep going around the track.

Ginny didn't just walk around the Franklin track. She ran, like someone was chasing her. Most of the time she kept to four or five miles, but every so often she'd double that, while listening to Green Day's "21 Guns" or "American Idiot."

Years passed, and Ginny grew accustomed to prison life at Franklin. She took college-level courses. She filed some legal briefs herself when she couldn't afford to pay her lawyers. And while she was devastated when the parole board denied her application, saying they didn't want her to come back for another ten years, Ginny took the news in stride. So many lifers in Ohio got shut down for fifteen, twenty years, sometimes more.

If she could just be patient. If she could apply the same diligence to her life that she did to her exercise regimen, maybe, just maybe, there would be a chance.

It took asking the right person the right question. But when Ginny asked it, boy, did it ever pay off.

...

Throughout the whole process of her trial and appeals, one man's testimony bothered Ginny the most. James Ferguson was the top toxicologist for all of Franklin County, working out of the County Coroner's Office, and he had been testifying as an expert at trials for what seemed like time immemorial. He seemed to have taken the witness stand as soon as he had graduated from The Ohio State University, which he said was in the early 1970s, maybe even before then.

That was the thing. The date of his graduation kept changing, depending on when Ferguson testified and what case it was. Of course Ginny didn't like what Ferguson said about her at trial. His testimony that the drugs in William's system increased while he was in the hospital, and that the increase was her direct fault, was devastating. In short, he testified that Ginny was not only *responsible* for her husband's death but that she had set out to kill him.

Over her time in prison Ginny learned that the facts that Ferguson recounted at her trial were flat-out wrong. She'd done her homework, consulting the Ohio legal code and finding a statute that a court could direct the coroner to change his decision about the cause, manner or mode of death already stated on a death certificate. A researcher working on behalf of her lawyer found William's hospital records. The antidepressants in William's system *decreased* while he was in the hospital, as was to be expected. The records also reported William was awake when admitted for the overdose. Ferguson had testified to William being in a coma. The more Ginny compared records with Ferguson's testimony at her trial, the more lies she uncovered.

What she didn't have was proof enough for the courts. Proof enough that would get them to listen. Ferguson was a seemingly unimpeachable witness, never wrong. How could she dent his armor?

Then, through a friend who had been through the system and was out on parole, Ginny found her way to

The Ohio State University alumni association's Web site. She found an e-mail address. She asked her friend to send them a message: Did James Ferguson attend the institution, as he had attested hundreds of times over decades of Franklin County criminal trials, and if so, when did he graduate?

Time passed, and Ginny finally got her answer from the university: Ferguson graduated from OSU in 1987. Just a year before William Lefever died. Just a year before Ginny's life turned into a Kafka tale. And at least fifteen years later than Ferguson claimed, over and over again, under oath.

Ginny pumped her fist in the air when she learned the news. The next time her feet pounded the ground as she circled the track at Franklin County Correctional, she knew she was running toward freedom.

Ginny Lefever's petition for habeas corpus, based on the discrediting of the testimony of James Ferguson, was granted in 2010. With no other convincing evidence, the court ordered that she be released from prison, more than twenty years after her original trial. Ginny sued the state of Ohio for compensation but has yet to receive any money. After a four-year battle to reclaim her nursing license, Ginny Lefever now works full time in the field near her home in Dublin, Ohio. She has a loving relationship with her son Alex and his family. As to the other children, she thinks, maybe someday, they won't be lost to her. She can wait as long as necessary. She's good at waiting.

———

SARAH WEINMAN is the editor of *Women Crime Writers: Eight Suspense Novels of the 1940s and 50s* (Library of America) and *Troubled Daughters, Twisted Wives: Stories from the Trailblazers of Domestic Suspense* (Penguin). Her work has appeared in the *New York Times*, the *Wall Street Journal*, the *Guardian*, *Ellery Queen Mystery Magazine* and *Alfred Hitchcock Mystery Magazine*, among other outlets. She lives in Brooklyn.

Editors' Note

According to a September 2014 study by the International Centre for Prison Studies, nearly a third of all female prisoners worldwide are incarcerated in the United States. The total population of females incarcerated in U.S. prisons and jails in 2013 was 213,700. Another study, by the Sentencing Project in 2007, points out that the number of women in prison increased between 1985 and 2007 at nearly double the rate of men, 404 percent versus 209 percent.

Women in prison have problems different from men. Bureau of Justice statistics show that incarcerated women experience sexual victimization by other inmates at a rate more than two-and-a-half times greater than men. Nearly three-quarters (73.1 percent) of women in state prisons in 2005 had a mental health problem, compared with 55 percent of men in prisons. Some of these issues are highlighted in the popular Web TV series *Orange is the New Black*.

William Michael Dillon and Ellen Moscovitz

Chapter 11

THE BLOODY YELLOW SHIRT

OBTAINING HELP

William Dillon (Florida exoneree), *as*
told to **Phillip M. Margolin**

———

THERE IS AN old saw that says that a man who
represents himself in court has a fool for a client, but
who can you count on to represent you if everyone in the
system, from the police who investigated the crime to the
defense attorney who was supposed to have your back,
has let you down?

At Okeechobee prison, huge fans at the end of the corridor sucked in hot air from outside the prison and blew
it around the cells carrying with it the stench of urine,
sweat and feces. One of the few places in the prison
with air-conditioning was the library. On a fateful day
in 2006, more than two decades into serving time for a
murder he did not commit, William "Bill" Dillon was in

that library. By chance or fate or blind luck, as a result of being in that library, he discovered that he had one last chance at freedom. He also discovered that this doorway to freedom was closing fast and the only person he could still count on was William "Bill" Dillon.

On August 17, 1981, the body of forty-year-old James Dvorak was discovered in the brush near Canova Beach, Florida. He was nude and had been beaten to death. On the day Dvorak was murdered, a truck driver named John Parker picked up a hitchhiker near the beach. Parker said that the light in the truck was dim but he could make out the hitchhiker's general appearance. The hitchhiker was wearing a bloody yellow T-shirt with the words "Surf It" on the front. Parker drove to a tavern three miles away and performed oral sex on the hitchhiker. Later that morning, after dropping off the hitchhiker, Parker found the bloody shirt in his truck. He threw it into a grocery store trash can.

Parker saw coverage of the murder on the news and called the police to tell them about the hitchhiker. He said that the hitchhiker was sweaty and had blood smeared on his leg and shorts in addition to the shirt. Later that day the police found the bloody T-shirt and other evidence including the victim's clothing.

The Pelican tavern was located near the crime scene. Five days after the murder, at six in the evening, Bill Dillon and his brother Joe were parked across the street from the tavern in the Canova Beach parking lot watching the waves. Their plan was no more complicated than crossing the street to shoot pool but it took a wrong turn when Bill was questioned by the police. The case had been reported in the news so Bill knew facts that had been revealed to the public, but the police were suspicious about Bill's "knowledge." They photographed him and asked him to report to the station house so he could help them with their investigation. Bill agreed to come in the next morning. When he didn't show up, they found him and brought him in. Then they charged him with first-degree murder.

Bill pled not guilty. At Bill's trial the state presented four key witnesses in an attempt to convict him. John Parker, who was legally blind in one eye, identified Bill as the hitchhiker.

Donna Parrish, a casual girlfriend, testified that she was with Bill on the night of the murder and remembered him standing over the victim's body while wearing the "Surf It" T-shirt. However, Parrish had changed her statements several times and recanted her testimony less than two weeks after the trial. She said she fabricated her testimony because she had been threatened with twenty-five years in prison as an accessory if she didn't testify against Bill. What's more, she said she'd had sex with the lead investigator, who was suspended for the incident and resigned.

John Preston was brought in to help with the investigation. He claimed to be an expert in handling scent-tracking dogs. At trial, he testified that "Harass II," his German shepherd, had linked the crime to the bloody shirt and the shirt to Bill. Preston claimed that his dog had tracked and connected Bill's scent to the crime scene even though a hurricane had washed the crime scene clean a week before.

Two years after Bill's conviction in late 1981, Preston was discredited. An Arizona Supreme Court justice called him a charlatan, and that state overturned all convictions that featured his testimony. A *20/20* report labeled him a fraud, someone who had not only invented his own credentials as an "expert," but also falsified his reports, creating "evidence" out of whole cloth.

Finally, Roger Dale Chapman, a jailhouse snitch, testified that Bill had confessed to him, but several details of the alleged confession did not fit the crime and no other inmate heard the alleged confession. After Bill's trial, prosecutors dropped sexual battery charges that had been filed against Chapman. Nearly thirty years later, Chapman admitted that prosecutors had coerced his testimony.

Bill testified that he was miles away when Dvorak was murdered and produced witnesses who corroborated his alibi, but he was convicted anyway after a five-day trial and sentenced to life in prison. In the five years following his conviction, all of Bill's appeals were denied.

In the spring of 2006, almost twenty-five years after his conviction, Bill was in the library at Okeechobee prison when an elderly African American inmate appeared in front of him. Bill had seen him in the law library where the man worked as a law clerk, dispensing legal advice to his fellow inmates. Out of the blue, the man asked Bill if he'd ever had a DNA test. Bill had heard of these tests but didn't understand how they would apply to him. After the man explained the science behind DNA testing, Bill wondered if any of the evidence from his case still existed. The man gave him a form he could use to request a DNA test and told him to file it in Brevard County where he was tried. It sounded like a long shot but Bill knew that his DNA would not be on the "Surf It" T-shirt if the shirt could be located. He was desperate and willing to try anything that could get him out of prison.

Then the old inmate told him something that almost made him lose hope.

"You've got to get on it, man," the clerk said. "A week from now, the Florida legislature is going to pass a new statute that will shut down all DNA testing in Florida. After June 6, no more requests for DNA testing will be accepted."

It was May 30 and Bill had a week to fill out his paperwork. In an ideal world, Bill would have had the money to hire a first-class defense attorney but that was not a possibility so Bill spent the next week learning how to become his own attorney. His research turned up two cases that were eerily similar to his own. In each case, a man tried in Brevard County had been convicted based on the testimony of John Preston and the evidence uncovered by his "magic" dog. Moreover, each case had involved a jailhouse snitch who testified that the defendant had confessed while behind bars. What really upset Bill was that many of the same people in the sheriff's department and the state's attorney's office who had been involved in his case had also been involved in these other cases. But there was also good news: both men had eventually been released from prison.

Up against time, Bill cobbled together a handwritten motion summarizing the facts of his case and explaining why he should be granted DNA testing. He filed the motion on June 6, just beating the clock.

Two months later, in August, Bill was transferred to his seventh prison, Hardee Correctional Institution in Bowling Green. In early October, Bill was working in the yard that contained a large, square, treeless cow pasture fenced in by barbed wire fences with a tower at three of the corners in which a thousand men roamed the grass and dirt paths. Bill was discouraged about the possibility of clearing his name when he got a callout for legal mail. Judge W. David Dugan had written Bill to inform him that he had received Bill's motion and was requiring the state to show just cause why Bill shouldn't be allowed to test the bloody T-shirt for DNA. Bill was stunned.

"What does this mean?" he asked Nate Johnson, an old friend he had met years earlier in another prison.

Johnson studied the letter. Then he smiled and waved

the letter in the air. "This is good, Bill," Johnson said, his voice filled with joy. "The judge is making the state say why you shouldn't get the DNA test. You're knocking on the door, Bill. You're knocking on the door."

On November 6, the state filed a confusing counterargument. Bill wrote a rebuttal and sent it to Judge Dugan. Once again, he set out all of the details of his conviction. A week later, Bill was astonished to learn that Judge Dugan had granted him a hearing. He reread the judge's letter as his hands holding it trembled with excitement. He set the letter down on his bunk and remembered the older African American from the law library in Okeechobee. It was hard to believe that the old man wasn't an angel sent to him by a higher power.

Bill received assistance from the Innocence Project of Florida. Officials determined that all of the physical evidence in Bill's case had been destroyed, with one exception—the yellow T-shirt. DNA testing showed that the blood on the shirt belonged to the victim but it also showed that Bill had not worn it. Biological material of someone other than Bill or the victim was found on the collar and in the armpit of the shirt but Bill's DNA was not found anywhere on the shirt.

On November 18, 2008, after being wrongly incarcerated for twenty-seven years, Bill was released from prison and all charges against him were dropped. For the first time in two and a half decades, Bill had not relied on a stranger to do his legal work. He had taken matters into

his own hands and, for the first time, Bill felt that he had
a competent attorney—himself.

*After his release, Brevard County investigators contin-
ued to harass Bill and manufactured doubts about his
innocence in the media to shield themselves from litigation and the shame of their own wrongdoing. Despite
these attempts to discredit Bill, the Florida legislature,
with support from Governor Rick Scott, awarded him
compensation.*

*Bill spent his initial years of freedom working at an
auto shop and keeping to his room. He would wake up
at the same time every morning and would not eat until
told that he could. But this story has a happy ending. In
March 2009, Bill attended an Innocence Conference in
Houston and met Ellen Moscovitz, the head of a DNA
testing company. They fell in love and eventually settled
in Chapel Hill, North Carolina.*

*Bill founded the William Dillon Freedom
Foundation that helps educate and support exonerees.
Ellen encouraged Bill to pursue music, and he launched
a music career. His solo album,* Black Robes and
Lawyers, *came out in August 2011. It drew compar-
isons with vintage Johnny Cash and received national
publicity on the* Today *show and* Fox and Friends.
*Bill also plays and tours with the Exoneree Band and
sang the National Anthem at a Tampa Bay Rays base-
ball game.*

—

PHILLIP M. MARGOLIN is a former criminal defense attorney with an extensive background in both trial and appellate work. Since 1996, Phillip has been a full-time writer. He is the author of more than twenty best-selling mysteries and thrillers, many of which involve trials. He is also the founder of Chess for Success, a nonprofit educational program for elementary and middle school children. He lives in Portland, Oregon.

Editors' Note

Forensic science has long been a bulwark of the U.S. justice system. Inspired in part by Sherlock Holmes and nineteenth- and early twentieth-century pioneers such as Alphonse Bertillon and Edmond Locard, Americans quickly took to the new techniques coming from Europe. Chester Gould's *Dick Tracy* explained scientific methods in comic strips, and television shows like *Quincy, M.E.* made the subject popular. However, deductions à la Sherlock Holmes are often incorrect. The base on which forensic science now rests is the American crime laboratory. There were 411 publicly funded labs in 2009, handling over four million requests for analysis. Many of these were underfunded and poorly supervised. Although national accreditation was introduced in 1984 and over 80 percent were accredited, almost 20 percent remain unaccredited.

In 2009, only 60 percent of publicly funded crime labs employed at least one forensic examiner who was externally certified by a certification body, such as the American Board of Criminalistics, International Association for Identification or the Forensic Toxicologist Certification Board, and in some jurisdictions, no professional training is required to be elected to the office of chief medical examiner or coroner. Even accreditation or training is not a guarantee of success: for example, a recent scandal in Florida, resulting in the tainting of dozens of cases, involved a corrupt employee of an accredited lab.[1]

"Bad science" (improper handling of materials, improper use of equipment, misinterpretation of analyses or outright fraud or ineptitude) was the basis of over 22 percent of the exonerations recorded in the National Registry of Exonerations. As television shows like *CSI*, *NCIS*, *The Mentalist* and others continue to grow in popularity, the public's belief in the infallibility of the forensic scientist is likely to result in more and more convictions based on "scientific proof." Bill Dillon's case involved a dog-sniffing "expert" that played a significant role in wrongfully convicting several exonerees.

---

1   http://www.businessinsider.com/forensic-csi-crime-labs-disaster-2014-4.

Jeff Deskovic. © Andy Marcus / Fred Marcus Photography

12.

THE LONG WAIT

LEGAL APPEALS

Jeff Deskovic (New York exoneree),
as told to **Gary Phillips**

———

FOR THE WRONGLY imprisoned, their biggest enemy is time itself. The minutes and hours drained from their real lives—the lives they enjoyed outside, before conviction—are forever lost. Their sense of themselves erodes, as the system crushes them into routine. By daily denying them any preferences or even the smallest choices about their lives, the system reminds them that they are worthless, merely bodies quarantined safely away from society. For some, the bright flame of their innocence can light the way through this endless darkness, but rarely can they allow themselves to experience unabashed hope.

"You're going home tomorrow."

He blinked, then shook his head to try and clear it.

He didn't want to get his hopes up today. Couldn't allow himself to fully believe the words of his lawyer, Nina Morrison. After all these years, after so many disappointments and setbacks, he'd long ago learned not to project too far ahead, not get caught up in "what if" and "what could be."

Jeffrey Mark Deskovic waited in the visitors area, not willing to accept what might be a different future. Even getting the Innocence Project's help hadn't been easy. More than a decade before, he'd written to them, trying to get the organization interested in his case, but they couldn't take him on. Back then, their primary focus was making sure an applicant's DNA had been tested and compared with the evidence from the scene of the crime, and because that had been done in Jeff's case, they couldn't work with him. Jeff was now seeking more sophisticated retesting of the pertinent physical evidence that had been collected and preserved.

Routinely, District Attorney Jeanine Pirro had fought all of his requests and appeals. Now, as Jeff sat in the Sing Sing visitors room, he wondered if finally—after sixteen years of keeping his hopes for justice under control—he might soon have reason to celebrate.

He'd been sent away to prison at age seventeen, and all seven of his appeals had been rejected. After he'd done his minimum time, he was summarily turned down for parole. Was it possible that at age thirty-three, freedom was finally beckoning to him?

...

Jeff's nightmarish odyssey began when he was sixteen years old, a quiet high school student who should have been worried about things like studying for his driver's test or hanging out with his friends. In 1990, the police in his hometown of Peekskill, New York, had arrested him for the rape and strangulation murder of his classmate Angela Correa. Alternately, the police would buddy up to Jeff or bully and cajole him, one of the officers telling him he'd better come clean, that he couldn't hold off the others from beating him if he didn't. With no parent or lawyer present, the minor was given three lie detector tests on one day at a private facility administered by a Putnam County sheriff's investigator. Jeff was told he'd failed those tests. He was kept hungry and tired and off balance. The authorities eventually obtained a false confession from the scared and confused teenager. When he did this, he did it mostly so they'd let him go home like they'd said they would. They didn't keep their promise.

Tried as an adult, Jeff was convicted of first-degree rape and second-degree murder, even though the DNA testing proved that the semen and hair samples recovered from the victim's body weren't his. Truths the police and the assistant district attorney managed to fit into their own version of the events during his trial. The gravity of his situation socked Jeff in the gut when the judge's gavel banged down.

"Maybe you are innocent," said Judge Nicholas

Colabella coldly to the stunned teenager. However, he explained, the jury had found him guilty, and the court was bound by its verdict. Jeff was sentenced to fifteen years to life and sent to the Elmira Correctional Facility, known as the "Hill," a maximum security state prison that ironically had been hailed as revolutionary when it opened in 1876, with its announced mission being to offer reform resources for its prisoners.

On its surface, prison life seemed to be monotonous and orderly: The morning bell would ring at 6:30 a.m., then you got ready for the live count ten minutes later. At 7:00, another bell would ring, and the prisoners were released to the mess hall for breakfast. Afterward, it was time for either your educational, vocational or therapeutic activity. At 11 a.m., back to your cell for an hour to perhaps read or rest or do jailhouse exercises in the tight space, such as sit-ups and push-ups, each rep another way to burn minutes off your long time down. Maybe you had "crackhead soup" in your cell before the noon lunch—ramen noodles, which even by prison wages were cheap to purchase in the commissary—instead of waiting for whatever was on the day's menu. Your afternoon work might mirror your morning tasks. At 3:45, you went back to your cell until dinnertime, 5 p.m. Afterward, you had rec time with an alternating group of half of the prisoners. You could play cards or checkers (chess was Jeff's game), shoot hoops, watch sports on TV, use the phone, work out or just take a shower.

You could lull yourself into believing that by minding your own business, everything would be copacetic. That was far from the truth: The prison gangs, often affiliated by race or religion, could create trouble for nonmembers. Or there were those individual inmates who preyed on other inmates. You had to constantly be aware of your surroundings. You also had to pay attention to the guards: When some of them were working, a prisoner had to try to avoid attracting their attention; otherwise they might choose to make your life miserable. Jeff later reflected, "Prison was a nonstop obstacle course in which the guards, staff and other prisoners were all potential obstacles to regaining one's freedom. Violence, and the threat of violence, permeated the atmosphere."

Despite this charged environment, he continued to believe that one day his innocence would be proved. He knew the massive size of the rock he was pushing uphill. There was no physical evidence against Jeff; his conviction was based solely on his purported confession—a confession based in part on crime scene details fed to him by the detectives who'd hammered at him back then, a confession that left him sobbing and curled beneath the table in a fetal position. Evidence that might have exculpated him had been mischaracterized. Semen *that was not Jeff's* had been found on the victim, but the prosecutor explained it away, claiming that it belonged to a male who'd been a consensual sex partner. Jeff, the prosecutor asserted, was jealous of this boyfriend, and that's what led him to commit his vengeful act.

And yet, stuck inside, Jeff persisted. He analyzed the legal documents generated by his case, deconstructing the arguments into their strengths and weaknesses. He studied the cases of other wrongful convictions that had been reversed, paying attention to what worked in their cases to obtain their freedom and maybe adapt one of those strategies to use in his matter as well. Such readings gave him a psychological boost, vicariously celebrating those who had gained their freedom. He could take himself away, imagining the exonerated walking through that steel door to the outside, to their families and loved ones, and being able to tell their side of the story.

Jeff found additional ways that he also used to defeat his imprisonment. In addition to the law books he combed, he read novels he had come upon while browsing in the prison library. He read them as another way to transport himself through the pages to a better place, if only for those relatively fleeting moments when engrossed in a book. One day, his now-regular escape into fiction was challenged by a trustee who worked in the library. The trustee urged him to read nonfiction works beyond the legal tomes.

Jeff embraced the idea and began reading books on presidential histories, self-help, relationships and so forth to broaden his mind. He even got hooked on sports radio shows, a kind of lifeline to the outside where he could listen to discussions like when pro football players would get into serious trouble with the law, and the debate was whether they should still be allowed to play. Often picking a book at random, he found himself one day thumbing through *Chicken Soup for the Prisoner's Soul, 101 Stories to Open the Heart and Rekindle the Spirit of Hope, Healing and Forgiveness*. Another book, *The Warden Wore Pink* by Tekla Dennison Miller, was excerpted in one of the *Chicken Soup* chapters. Miller had been a trailblazing warden at the Huron Valley Women's Prison and the men's facility as well. Her comments on the system resonated with Jeff. She seemed like a progressive-minded person who might be a resource.

The *Chicken Soup* book provided contact information for some of the authors in the collection, including Biddle Publishing. He wrote a letter to Miller in care of the publisher, hoping that the former warden would know someone or some agency that would help him.

Over the years, he'd written to other publishers and organizations, in the hope that someone would listen to his story. This time someone did, and an employee at Biddle passed along his letter to an investigator named Claudia Whitman (instead of Miller). She wrote back to Jeff and suggested that he again try the Innocence Project. While she was aware that he'd previously tried to get their interest, she noted that due to the advancement of DNA technology, their prior reason for turning him down no longer applied. Obtaining results from the new

DNA database could provide newly discovered evidence that could be used to overturn his conviction.

Okay, Jeff reasoned, he'd roll those dice again. He liked that Whitman had bullet pointed the facts of Jeff's case in a dossier and she was able to use the dossier to recruit others (such as the New York State Defenders Association) to also write letters of support to the Innocence Project, urging them to take his case. For half a year the Innocence Project debated internally about his case. Each time they decided "no," Jeff would later find out, their intake worker, Maggie Taylor, went to the mat for him. After each refusal, she would regroup and present another course of action on Jeff's case, arguing how new testing could be used to exonerate him. Jeff had raised the fact that there was now a New York State DNA database that could be used in order to try to identify the actual killer—which would, of course, also prove Jeff's innocence. Finally, they decided in his favor and took up his plight.

Fortunately, there was also a different DA on the scene in New York's Westchester County, Janet DiFiore. Her office agreed to the new, more sophisticated DNA testing that previously Pirro wouldn't allow. Once again it confirmed that the physical evidence found on the victim didn't match Jeff. Even more important, the new test results were entered into the then recently compiled New York State DNA data bank. A match came back implicating Steven Cunningham—a man who was already doing time for strangling his girlfriend to death. He'd been imprisoned three and a half years after Jeff had been sent away. The state's consensual sex theory went up in smoke, replaced by a very real perpetrator.

"Maybe you are innocent." Those words said coolly by Judge Nicholas Collabella before sentencing him had never left Jeff.

After serving nearly a decade and a half at Elmira Correctional Facility, Jeff had been transferred to the more infamous Sing Sing maximum security prison as the new testing was done and reconfirmed. That day in the Sing Sing visitors area, Nina Morrison, the lawyer sent from the Innocence Project, told him, after pleasant-ries, "You're going home tomorrow."

"No, I'm not," an incredulous Jeff said.

"Yes, you are," she insisted. They went back and forth like that three times, and even after that it took Jeff quite a bit of time to eventually believe it.

The next day, shackled and cuffed, Jeff rode in the van to his appointed courtroom at the Westchester County Courthouse in White Plains. The irony of still being con-fined wasn't lost on Jeff as mere yards away, he watched people free to go about their daily walk or drive through the vehicle's windows. "It was like a parallel world out there," Jeff remembered.

After being freed that September, finally on November 2, 2006, all charges against Jeff were dismissed, and it was publicly acknowledged he'd been wrongly convicted. The press conference Jeff had dreamed about so many times became a reality as he stood on the steps of the courthouse. "I am not standing here in front of you because of the system, I am standing here in front of you despite the system," he said.

Jeff would make several more trips to that courthouse in White Plains, eventually witnessing Cunningham's sentencing. He'd admitted to raping and killing Angela Correa. As reported in the *New York Times*, Angela's mother told Jeff, "How I would like to turn back time and return to you what was cruelly taken away."

Jeffrey Deskovic received compensation from the state of New York, Westchester County and the city of Peekskill. In 2011, he started The Jeffrey Deskovic Foundation for Justice, the mission of which is to exonerate the wrongfully convicted, prevent wrongful convictions by raising awareness and seeking legislative changes and help exonerees reintegrate back into society. In 2013, Jeff received a master's degree from the John Jay College of Criminal Justice. He frequently lectures about wrongful convictions, makes media appearances, and gives commentary, writes articles and lobbies elected officials and testifies at legislative hearings. In recognition of his advocacy work, Jeff won the New Yorker of the Week award from NY 1 News in December 2014 and the Humanitarian of the Year award from the New Rochelle Chamber of Commerce on April 20, 2015. He is certi-

fied as an instructor in New Jersey's Police Academies, participating in the ethics portion of the training, while he has also given numerous presentations at judicial seminars on wrongful conviction topics such as "Catching and Correcting Wrongful Convictions in the Normal Course of the Appellate Process," "How Proceduralism Has Hindered Substantive Justice," "Dealing with Postconviction Motion Claims of Actual Innocence" and "Avoiding Presiding over a Wrongful Conviction."

———

Among **GARY PHILLIPS**'s previous endeavors, which included delivering dog cages and repairing scaffolds, he was the communications director for the Legal Aid Foundation of Los Angeles. He's written more than a dozen mystery novels, edited several anthologies and published numerous short stories. He is the former chapter president of the SoCal Chapter of the Mystery Writers of America and vice president of the Private Eye Writers of America.

Editors' Note

DNA testing, as noted above, is a factor in less than a fourth of the wrongful convictions nationwide, so it is not the "magic bullet" of exonerations. In fact, in a number of sexual assault convictions later overturned, DNA testing was actually done in the underlying cases and showed the defendant was not a match to the DNA samples found. Prosecutors, in those cases, often argued that the victim must have had consensual sex *before* being sexually assaulted. Jeff Deskovic's was one such case, as was Juan Rivera's, featured in the last chapter, in which the victim was an eleven-year-old child whose identical twin testified, denying that they were sexually active.

Antione Day, center, with exonerees Jovan Mosley, left, and Marvin Reeves

13.

THE LAST BAD MORNING

EXONERATION

Antione Day (Illinois exoneree),
as told to **Jamie Freveletti**

ANTIONE DAY WAS imprisoned for a murder and attempted murder that he did not witness and for which he was ultimately found completely innocent by the court that convicted him. When he was released, Antione learned that while imprisonment was terrible, release from prison was not the end of his troubles. He learned, firsthand, how little "justice" is afforded an exoneree upon release, and how freedom is just the beginning.

Antione Day's first glimmer of hope appeared six years into a ten-year nightmare and came in the form of a soon-to-be-retired real estate lawyer named Howard Joseph. Fingered by false witness testimony, Antione, a twenty-eight-year-old former rhythm-and-blues drummer, was convicted for a murder and shooting that even one of the surviving victims denied Antione had committed. Sentenced to the Pontiac Correctional Center for sixty years, Antione began a hellish existence, locked up with some of the worst that humanity had to offer.

Pontiac is a high-security prison. Only the worst inmates stay there. Murderers, rapists. Located two hours from Chicago, it's a vintage redbrick building surrounded by concertina wire. Gang members filled the prison. A riot claimed the lives of three guards, and ten years later a supervisor was stabbed to death in the South cell block in a contract killing ordered by a gang member.

Antione was in the East cell house, a classic prison configuration with five tiers of cells running along cat-walks. The cell house held almost 360 prisoners, guarded by five jumpy prison guards all well aware they were outnumbered. A guard stood in a high corner and held an automatic weapon. Bullet holes peppered the nearby concrete where the guard would shoot his initial warn-ing shots. Signs in the prison yard gave the excellent advice: SIT DOWN when shots are fired.

Fights broke out at all times of the day and night, and when they did the entire facility would be put on lockdown. Antione would be confined to his cell "twenty-three and one," meaning twenty-three hours of every day with one hour free. But often even that one hour would come and go with everyone still locked inside.

Many of the cells didn't have bars, but instead a steel

door with a narrow opening at chest height that allowed meals to be passed to the prisoner. The regular sounds of daily life never reached Antione. Not the sound of cars on a road, birds in the trees or planes overhead. The rising of the sun and its transition to dark was impossible to determine. The monotony of long hours with nothing to do, nothing to see and nothing to hear would take its toll on most men in lockdown. After a while the mind begins to crumble. For a man who spent his life creating the melodies and sounds that lift the spirits and capture the soul, the interminable days left him empty and in danger of unending despair.

But Antione didn't break easily. He would pound out his sadness in song and let the music transport him to a place where no one could reach him. Antione knew that if he was to retain any portion of himself he needed to reconnect with the person he'd been, and so he requested that he be allowed to play music during his free hour. The problem: Pontiac Correctional facility used to have musical instruments, but no longer did. Undeterred, Antione wrote a letter of request to Superintendent Daniel Kelly.

Then, another fight broke out and an inmate was stabbed. Pontiac went back on lockdown, but this lockdown was one of the worst. Antione stayed in his cell for thirty days straight.

Antione's essential belief that justice would return him to freedom never wavered. He was the fifth of seven children, and his mother was his rock and music his freedom. He refused to walk around prison talking up his innocence, like so many prisoners who claimed they were but weren't. Instead he held his knowledge close. He believed that his spirit would not allow him to be incarcerated forever. He had an unshakeable belief that he would one day be exonerated, but as the days became years that belief was tested. His postconviction appeal was denied, and it appeared as though he would spend the rest of his life in prison.

Antione spent his waking hours during the thirty-day lockdown busting out push-ups and reading Malcolm X and Marcus Garvey and others who had fought the fight and survived. When the doors finally opened the guards handed Antione a letter. The supervisor had granted his request. Musical instruments would be provided, as well as an hour of rehearsal time.

Antione rounded up other inmates who could play guitars or sing or rap, and a jailhouse band formed. They were led into a chapel of sorts, with a stage and space to rehearse. The drum kit was a battered set from who knows where, but when Antione began to play he felt again the driving life force of music.

Bob Marley once said, "One good thing about music, when it hits you, you feel no pain." Antione pounded away his pain on the battered old drum set, holding back the desolation of his everyday existence and fueling his ferocious spirit. That set kept him going for a few more

years, but the toll of incarceration, with its mindless rit-
uals and numbing boredom, still chewed his edges.

One morning, a guard told him that he had a visitor
and led him into the visiting room. Antione walked in
and stood in front of a little old white man he'd never
seen before. A thick glass partition separated them.

"I'm your lawyer. Please sit down," Howard Joseph
said. "I've been reading your file, and I know what they
did to you. I'm going to get you out. You ready to go
home?"

Antione said he was. And he sat down.

...

The soul-crushing monotony and rigidity of incarcerated life continued.

Court day in a prison is simply another opportunity
to control the prisoners and enforce rules that seem to
exist only to cement bureaucratic inefficiency. It begins
at three o'clock in the morning, when hundreds of prisoners are pulled out of bed and forced to line up to begin
the long march to the courtrooms of the judges who
are handling their cases. These prisoners wait, shackled
to each other, standing shoulder to shoulder in holding
areas, some for over ten hours, before they are waved
into a room for a hearing that lasts for only a few minutes. When it's over, the prisoners reenter the line and
begin their long return to jail.

The next years created a cycle of expectation and

devastation for Antione. Every time a hearing was scheduled, he'd be greeted by Joseph.

"You ready to go home?"

"Yes, I am."

It became their mantra.

They'd head into the courtroom, an unlikely pair, the African American rhythm-and-blues musician convicted of murder, and the elderly attorney in a crooked tie given to wearing corduroy moccasin house slippers and a rumpled trench coat. Antione often thought of Joseph as his own personal angel, a title that Joseph insisted Antione not use. But angels come in many guises, and Joseph had all the hallmarks of the real deal.

The hearing would commence, the other side would ask for a continuance and the process would drag on further. Antione would be bundled back into the bus for the long ride to the jail, but before he would leave, Joseph would urge Antione to keep the faith, that to overturn a conviction took time and to know that they would prevail. Antione continued to pound out his music during his free hour, but his faith was spreading thin.

Reversing Antione's nightmare, or "kidnapping" as he preferred to call it, hinged on Antione's lawyer's failure to present or interview alibi witnesses and incorrectly coaching the witnesses he did call. Even though one of the surviving victims told the court that Antione was not the shooter, Antione was convicted. Joseph would later use the lawyer's ineffective assistance to overturn the wrongful conviction.

But even reversing the conviction didn't lead to immediate release, because the state is given great latitude and time to decide whether to retry the case. In some cases it can take years. For Antione, he was transferred to Cook County lockup for seven months while he waited for their decision.

On May 8, 2002, a guard came to Antione's cell, woke him up and told him that he was scheduled for court. Antione hadn't been informed, but he lined up for the long, shuffling walk to the courthouse at Chicago's 26th and California. He shuffled onto a transport bus and was shuttled into a holding area. He entered the courtroom to find Joseph and the prosecutors there.

The judge looked up and said, "Mr. Day, do you want to go home today?"

Antione smiled at the judge's version of Joseph's question, and, thinking nothing of it, said, "Yes, Your Honor, I do."

The judge signed an order and handed it to the clerk. "Congratulations, Mr. Day."

Antione Day was free.

Stunned, Antione walked out of the courtroom to begin the long discharge process, which, due to the antiquated system still in place in Cook County, could take as long as ten hours. Antione's discharge took eight.

Joseph stayed with him for a while, but as the discharge dragged on he eventually had to leave to deal with other matters.

After the endless paper pushing and vetting, Antione, still in his prison uniform, was led to a large room filled from floor to ceiling with the discarded clothes of hundreds of people who had traded their clothing for a jail uniform. The room smelled like a combination of sweat and dirt and old shoes.

The guard waved at the pile. "You want to go home, then you need to put these on."

The clothes weren't cleaned, cataloged or in any other way organized. Antione grabbed a large pair of sweatpants and an oversized shirt, with sleeves that hung over his hands, and put them on. The odor from the clothes nearly overwhelmed him. Exhausted, hungry and smelling like a wild animal, the guards walked him outside to the corner of 26th and California, on the tough West Side of Chicago. And left him there.

It was early evening. Cold and rainy with dismal skies. Antione hadn't been offered a chance to call his family, his last forty-three dollars in his account was back at the main jail, and he had no cell phone, no transit card and no way to get home. He stood in the rain, dazed, while he stared at the passing cars, free of shackles, free of his prison jumpsuit, free for the first time in a decade.

An hour passed, then two, and still Antione stood

there. The rain soaked his borrowed clothes and the cars whizzed by. After ten years of regimented life he was free to go anywhere, but was too stunned to get there. The prison system kidnapped him, stripped him of everything he had, held him for ten years, and when they were done spit him back out without any means to buy a bus pass, make a call or get directions to a facility where he could sleep. Even the clothes on his back weren't his own. And night was falling on the sketchy West Side of Chicago.

Then another remarkable event occurred. A car pulled up, and the driver lowered the window, stuck his head out and stared at Antione in amazement.

"Antione? Antione Day?" It was a friend of Antione's from long ago. "What are you doing out here?"

"I busted out," Antione said.

The man paused, then both laughed.

"Get in and I'll drive you home."

Antione got in the car, and his friend Anthony, who hadn't seen him in years, took him to his home, let him take a shower, brought him some clean clothes that fit and then offered Antione his phone to call his mother. Antione didn't tell her he was coming home, just that he loved her and would see her soon. A few hours later she screamed as he walked into her house a free man.

Antione spent two weeks at his mother's side, wrapped in her love and soaking in the fact that he was free.

Antione Day received a Certificate of Innocence in September 2010. After initially working construction jobs, he eventually obtained a position as an outreach coordinator of prison reentry at the Howard Area Community Center, where he mentored at-risk teenagers and parolees as well as ran neighborhood stabilization and antiviolence programs. Antione also started the Life After Justice Center with Jarrett Adams, which aims to help those who are exonerated reenter society and the lives they were torn from when convicted. They're raising funds and searching for a home on the West Side of Chicago to house these exonerees for the time they need to acclimate again to freedom.

Antione now works for the Better Boys organization and is a member of the Exoneree Band, all exonerated musicians.

Howard Joseph died in the years following Antione's release, and his son gave Antione his father's law license. Antione framed it and it hangs on a wall in his house. Every year, Life After Innocence gives an award in Joseph's name to someone who works for the innocence world without recognition or compensation.

Antione never got his forty-three dollars back from his prison account.

———

JAMIE FREVELETTI is the internationally and number one Amazon best-selling, ITW and Barry Award–winning author of the Emma Caldridge series. In addition to her own books, the estate of Robert Ludlum has asked her to write for his Covert One series. Her latest for the series, *The Geneva Strategy*, was released in February 2015. She lives in Chicago with her family.

Editors' Note

The Sixth Amendment of the Bill of Rights (the U.S. Constitution) establishes the right to assistance of counsel for individuals accused of crimes, and it has long been the law that states must provide representation for indigent defendants. However, Congress has not created either a national standard for the quality of the defense provided nor funding, leaving many states with inadequate, underfunded systems.[1] As a result, many defendants find themselves represented by overburdened and sometimes incompetent defense lawyers, with little or no funding available for proper defense investigation. Note that the problem of inadequate legal defense is not limited to defendants with public defenders; many of the complaints included members of the private bar.

According to a report by the Innocence Project,[2] the

---

1   See the National Right to Counsel Committee report, "Justice Denied: America's Continuing Neglect of Our Constitutional Right to Counsel" (The Constitution Project, 2009).

2   *Court Findings of Ineffective Assistance of Counsel Claims in Post-Conviction Appeals Among the First 255 DNA Exoneration Cases*, September 2010.

most common types of claims in successful exonerations included defense lawyers who failed to present defense witnesses (often to establish/confirm an alibi), failed to seek DNA testing or have serology testing done to try to exclude the client, failed to object to prosecutor arguments or to evidence introduced by the state and failed to interview witnesses in preparation for trial or to cross-examine state witnesses. Other examples of less frequently reported claims included failure to investigate, failure to object to an identification and failure to present expert testimony. Some of the worst offenders among counsel were lawyers who slept in the courtroom during trial, appeared while intoxicated, were disbarred shortly after handling the defendant's case or simply failed to show up for hearings.

Only a few will be able to use "inadequate legal representation" as a grounds for overturning a conviction. In *Strickland v. Washington*,[3] the Supreme Court established a test to determine "ineffectiveness": (1) the counsel's representation must fall below an objective standard of reasonableness; and (2) there must be reasonable probability that, but for counsel's unprofessional errors, the result of the proceeding would have been different. Further, in determining whether the defense was inadequate, the Supreme Court stated that courts "must be highly deferential . . . A court must indulge

---

3   466 U.S. 668 (1984).

a strong presumption that counsel's performance was within the wide range of reasonable professional assistance." Nonetheless, more than one-fifth of the exonerations recorded in the National Registry of Exonerations included "inadequate legal defense" as a basis for overturning the conviction.

Jerry Miller, courtesy of the Innocence Project

14.

MOVING FORWARD

POSTRELEASE

Jerry Miller (Illinois exoneree),
as told to **John Mankiewicz**

———

FOR SOME VICTIMS *of wrongful conviction/incarceration, there comes a choice: Play nice, live a lie, publicly repent the crimes you didn't commit, do your time, maybe get paroled, but get out. Or be steadfast in your declarations of innocence, no matter what the cost. Jerry Miller served every minute of his time, almost twenty-six years, and was released on a punishing parole that was, at times, worse than prison. Somehow, through it all, he stayed strong and never stopped fighting for his innocence.*

APRIL 23, 2007
CHICAGO, ILLINOIS

Jerry Miller was worried. Late Sunday night, the night before his exoneration, and he couldn't sleep at all. Sure, the DNA test had cleared him, almost a month ago. And the Cook County state's attorney, persuaded by the evidence, had joined the motion for release. In just a few hours Jerry would walk into court a convicted rapist who had served his time—more than a year in county jail, twenty-four and a half years in Illinois state prisons, eleven months on parole—and walk out an innocent man. "Not just innocent," Jerry says now. "*Exonerated*. That's a good word. My innocence was *proven*. A scientific *fact*."

Jerry Miller was about to become the two hundredth person exonerated by the Innocence Project on DNA evidence. The Innocence Project lawyer, interns, everyone who'd worked on his case for the last year and a half had flown into Chicago for the hearing. Even Barry Scheck and Peter Neufeld, the big cheeses, the cofounders, were going to be there. First thing in the morning, they would all meet at 26th and California, the Cook County Criminal Courts building. After court there would be a big press conference. Jerry's exoneration would launch a monthlong Innocence Project national campaign to address and prevent wrongful convictions. Then, a celebratory lunch for the lawyers, Jerry, his extended family, everyone involved. At Sullivan's, the Chicago steakhouse.

Still, the night before, at his cousin Karen Hicks's

house on the South Side, Jerry Miller was worried. It had been a long time since things had gone his way. "At seventeen," Jerry admits, "I was all over the place. High school had disrupted my ability to focus. I wanted to hang out, and I ended up hanging out with kids who wanted to cut school."

Growing up, Jerry had been very close to his grandparents. They lived in nearby London Town. He used to ride his bicycle to their house all the time. "Right when I was losing interest in school," Jerry remembers, "my grandmother passed. She was the first person close to me who died. She was the one who told me what to do. She always wanted me to push myself, do better."

Inspired by his grandmother, still only seventeen, Jerry enlisted in the U.S. Army. "It turned out she was right," Jerry says now. "The challenges, the discipline of the Army, I liked it. I matured a little. Enough to appreciate what it takes to be alone, on your own. To take responsibility for myself."

After three years in the Army, Jerry came home to Chicago and lived at his parents' house in Jeffrey Manor. When his Army savings ran out, he got a restaurant job. Jerry felt like he was getting traction on a good, solid start to his adult, civilian life. He felt comfortable inside himself. Confident. Excited about the future.

Then, although Jerry Miller didn't know it at the time, his future blew up. On the evening of September 16, 1981, while Jerry was home with his parents and brother watching Thomas "The Hitman" Hearns fight Sugar Ray Leonard on pay-per-view, the die was cast. At the same time, on the other side of town, a forty-four-year-old white female walked to her car, parked on the roof deck of a downtown Chicago garage. As she opened her car door, a young black man came out of nowhere, a blur of quick violence, shoving her into the car. He beat, robbed and raped her, forced her into the trunk and tried to drive out of the garage. Recognizing the victim's car, the cashier told the unfamiliar driver to back up. When another cashier approached, the rapist fled on foot and was gone.

This, of course, was a hot case in Chicago. *A black man raping a white woman?* There was tremendous pressure to solve the case, to make someone pay, close the books. The victim was so brutally raped and beaten that a rape kit exam could not be performed. She could not identify her attacker. A week later, working off a composite sketch created from descriptions by the two parking attendants, Chicago cops picked up Jerry Miller at his parents' house. He was picked out of a lineup by the attendants, charged, quickly tried and convicted. At sentencing, Judge Thomas J. Maloney, citing "overwhelming evidence," sentenced Jerry Miller, just twenty-two years old, to forty-five years in prison.

Now, after his long prison sentence and parole, on the eve of exoneration, Jerry was forty-seven years old. In prison, he'd written hundreds of letters to pro bono lawyers, organizations, anyone who could possibly help. When no one responded, Jerry filed his own appeals, two of them, assisted by jailhouse lawyers. The second time around, Jerry waited more than two years to get turned down by the appellate court. Then, while watching television in 2001, Jerry saw something about the Innocence Project in New York. He wrote them and kept writing, for four years, until the Innocence Project officially took his case, in 2005. In fact, when Jerry was released from prison in 2006, the Innocence Project was still looking for DNA evidence that could prove his innocence.

Due to the nature of his conviction, Jerry Miller was released from prison on a highly restrictive three-year parole. His first taste of freedom lasted only slightly longer than the bus ride home to his mother's house. The next day, parole officers showed up. "Five or six of them," Jerry says, "just in case the whole neighborhood didn't notice." They took him to a nearby police station, where a lieutenant major informed him, *for the first time*, that he'd have to register as a sex offender.

"They showed me the papers," Jerry says now. "I didn't *have* to sign. But if I *didn't*, they'd take me right back to prison. My choice."

Which, of course, one day out, was no choice at all. And, after Jerry signed the papers, there was more. As a registered sex offender, he had to attend sex offender *classes*. Weekly. Mandatory. And, oh yeah, he'd have to pay for them himself. Forty bucks a pop. "Man, I had done all this time," Jerry remembers, "and now I had to sit at a table with a bunch of *real* sex offenders while someone tried to cure me of my 'inclinations.' It was embarrassing. Demeaning."

Jerry shakes his head, remembering the cold hardness of those days. "Those classes could've broke me. I had to put my pride aside. I had to deal with the stigma. When they asked me to say something, I said the same thing I'd been telling everyone for twenty-five years. 'My name is Jerry Miller; I'm innocent of this crime, and I hope one day I'll be exonerated.'"

For the first ten months of parole, Jerry did everything he was supposed to do, everything that was asked. He moved to his cousin Karen's apartment on the South Side. He went to his classes, every single one. Paid for them, even when money was tight, which was *all the time*. He wore a humiliating GPS ankle bracelet, the thing that felt like a neon sign, a flashing arrow following him everywhere he went, telling the whole world to look out, beware, *this is a bad person*. And, because there was just one set of rules for all sex offenders, Jerry was the worst kind of bad person. *A child molester*.

For Jerry Miller, family was so important. For starters, his parents had been his biggest supporters. His father, Jemmar Miller—also Jerry; his son was "Little Jerry"—was a journeyman at Ford and a jack-of-all-trades, proficient at architecture, carpentry, "anything he put his mind to," Jerry says now. "My dad did everything possible for me. He was gonna put up our house for bail, but I wouldn't let him. It was too embarrassing. But he made sure I had a paid lawyer at the trial." When Jerry went away, his dad was the one who organized visits, piling Jerry's brothers and sister in the car with him, every week, making sure Jerry didn't lose touch with family, and vice versa.

"Exceptional, my old man was," says Jerry now. "When he died, in 1993, life got really difficult. In prison, you lose hope every day, and get it back every day. My dad helped me with my hope. I was broken up."

For Jerry Miller, the emotional pit of that loss seemed bottomless. "I had been fighting for myself, but when I lost my dad, I had to go through a change. I had to turn it around. I was in a dark, dark place. Then I thought, you know what? Let this fight be not just about *me*. Because when someone goes away for what I went away for, it hurts the whole family. I'd been trying to clear my name, my reputation. Then I decided to let the fight be about clearing my father's name, too. Which gave me another way to fight, brought me back up. My dad gave me a second wind."

Jerry's mom, Marion, was the one who gave Jerry his first tools to survive. In the beginning, before trial, when Jerry was in county jail, he talked to his mom on the phone. When his mom said he sounded depressed, Jerry asked what he should do.

"You get off the phone, right now," Marion Miller told her son, "and you read. You read, and don't stop reading."

Jerry laughs, remembering that phone call. "My whole life, every time my mother said something was gonna happen, it happened. So I read. I started out reading newspapers. I like sports, so I read the sports section. Then novels. Then I started reading things that mattered. Spiritual things. The Bible. And anything I read, I'd read it over and over until I understood it."

Naturally, while Jerry's life was frozen in prison, siblings and cousins had moved forward, married, had families of their own. Jerry heard about nieces and nephews as they were born. He saw pictures. Lived on secondhand stories of their childhoods. Now he was out, and the rules said *he couldn't be alone with kids.* Jerry endured this cascade of humiliations while working two jobs: a line cook at WoWo's, a barbecue joint nearby, and helping out Karen at YesWeCan, her transportation business that shuttled older folks around Chicago. At the same time, he was trying to integrate himself back into society, and it wasn't easy.

"I was twenty-one when the cops picked me up for questioning," Jerry points out. "A young man. I'd been incarcerated since the moment I got in that police car. When I got out, I was forty-seven years old. Naturally, I wanted to be with women. Attracting them, getting them interested, that was easy. But *then* what? As soon as you're sitting in that living room, that bedroom, you think, 'When do I tell her about my situation?' If you tell her at the start—'By the way, I'm a registered sex offender'—it's over before it begins. But you got to tell her. You've got to be honest. But you've got to find the right moment to give her the news. And," Jerry adds, "depending on how far I was from Karen's place, that moment better be before 8:30, or 8:45, because I had a 9 p.m. curfew."

For the first ten months on parole, while the Innocence Project worked his case, Jerry negotiated this impossible reentry into the civilized world and obeyed every single bullshit rule of his parole. The urine drops. The not going outside, *even to the backyard.* The orders to keep the house dark on Halloween, to not answer the door. Christ, the parole officers had even come by on Halloween night. Four of them, ringing the doorbell, testing him.

Jerry passed the test. He passed all the tests, but it was getting to him. "Emotionally, it was a difficult time. You think you have it figured out, but you don't. You can't. And it's nothing you can problem solve, because your whole life is based in emotion. Everything you see, everything you touch, the way people look at you, it's based on a *lie.* To be lied on is a tough thing. To be put before the world as someone I wasn't and carry that weight for twenty-five, twenty-six years is a very tough thing.

"It got to a point," Jerry admits now, "that I was within *hours* of telling them I was done. I couldn't do it anymore. I was going to make the call, tell them go ahead, take me back, I'll finish up in jail. I'd been abused by society, now society was treating me like a piece of shit. In jail, *everyone's* a piece of shit."

Jerry Miller remembers exactly when he hit the wall. When he was *this close* to giving up. March 28, 2007. An easy day to remember because, amazingly—or not, depending on your spiritual beliefs—it's the same day he heard from Colin Starger, the Innocence Project lawyer handling his case in New York. "In all those years," Jerry says now, "I had never given up to the point of *truly* giving up. But that day, I was *there*. I'm telling you, that call came right on time."

Starger asked if Jerry was sitting down, and then told him the big news. The same thing Jerry had been telling anyone who would listen for twenty-six years. The difference was, Starger had proof. The Innocence Project had tracked down a slip the victim had worn during the attack, and the Cook County prosecutor's office had agreed to DNA testing. Finally, the results were back, and Jerry had been excluded. He was innocent.

"Once I came down from the high of that phone call, I knew that was just phase one," Jerry explains. "I had the scientific part, the DNA. But I wanted a successful ending, and for that, I needed the human part, too. To me, that meant a lawyer from the other side, someone, a *human being*, telling me that the city of Chicago had been wrong."

Jerry Miller wanted an apology. A private, human

acknowledgment of what had been done to him. "I was so young, so naïve when this happened," he explains now. "From the time they picked me up for questioning, through the arrest, the trial, I didn't have a clue what was going down. I know, it's obvious now, looking back, but it took me *years* to put it together. And once I did, I wondered how they could do it? Not just to me, to anyone? It was like I wasn't even a person."

What Jerry Miller realized, inarguable after even a casual reading of the facts, is that the Chicago cops needed to solve this crime, and because Jerry had been stopped a week before, for walking while black, he was a convenient solution. With the name and address of a man who was the same color and general age of the man the two parking garage attendants had described, the Chicago justice system kicked into gear.

But there was one problem. At the exact time the rape occurred, Jerry Miller was miles away, watching a fight on pay-per-view with his parents and brother. With such a solid alibi, how could they even *arrest* Jerry Miller? "Welcome to racism in America," says Barry Scheck.

A week after the crime, the two cops who'd stopped Jerry Miller on the street saw the composite sketch of the suspect. Not troubled by the fact that Jerry had a full-grown goatee and the perp was clean shaven, those same two cops picked Jerry up for questioning. They took him to a police station seventeen miles away. They held him for seventy-two hours. They didn't let him make a phone call. They took his picture. They inked his right palm and asked him to place it on top of a garbage can lid. They took a blood sample. On the third day, the cops asked Jerry to take a lie detector test. "About what?" Jerry wondered. The cops would not say. Jerry said sure. "I knew I hadn't done anything," Jerry says now. "If I hadn't done anything, I really believed I had nothing to worry about."

Meanwhile, for close to three days, Jerry Miller's frantic parents looked all over town for their missing son. Called police stations, in a widening circle. Nothing.

The cops put Jerry in a car and drove him to another police station for the lie detector test. As the cops led Jerry inside, he saw his father's car pulling up. His mother, getting out. But his parents didn't see him.

Before Jerry took the lie detector test, the cops asked him to sign something. "It had some legal mumbo jumbo on the first page," Jerry remembers, "but the second page was mostly blank. They wanted me to sign on the bottom, under all that blank space. Which was a problem. Because one thing I'd learned in the Army was *never* sign anything you don't understand."

Jerry refused to sign, "and that was the first time the cops got mad. They said I *had* to sign it if I was going to take the lie detector test." The cops got angrier. They yelled. When Jerry continued to refuse to sign the bottom of a blank piece of paper, one of the cops said, "Fine. You can fight it in court."

The next day, a police van took Jerry Miller to 26th and California, where he was charged with the crime. He'd been taken in for questioning more than three days before, and this was the first time he heard the word "rape."

While Jerry Miller was waiting in Cook County jail for his trial, he saw the two parking garage attendants on television. "They were getting citizen awards from the city of Chicago," Jerry remembers. "For helping the police catch the suspect in a big rape case. I remember wondering why they didn't show my picture."

A Cook County security guard laughed. "You don't get it, youngblood," he explained. "These cops are shooting in the dark."

At the trial, no one mentioned Jerry Miller's partial palm print on the top of the garbage can, because it didn't match the print at the crime scene. No one mentioned Jerry Miller's blood because it was AB positive and the perp's was type O. Which makes sense. When you're shooting in the dark, you sometimes miss.

At Karen's house, the night before exoneration, "dizzy inside myself," Jerry Miller knew exactly what had been done to him. The casual, systemic racism of Chicago's justice system had stolen twenty-six years of his life, but Jerry knew he couldn't dwell on that. "I'm a positive person," he says now. "I had to be. In prison, you don't have time to waste time. You got to keep learning, move forward all the time. I was about to get my life back, and I knew I had to *keep* moving forward. I thought a personal apology would help me let that bitterness go."

As the sun came up over the South Side of Chicago on Monday morning, Jerry Miller was "worried about the day, how it would unfold. I *hoped* I'd get the apology, but I knew that wasn't up to me. The things you can't control? You can't let them control *you*." Jerry figured he'd done everything within his own power to prepare for the day. Since the DNA test came back, as plans were made for his exoneration, he'd kept in touch with the Innocence Project. Gone to his classes. Obeyed all the rules. Yesterday, Sunday, he'd gone to church, then to his cousin Lance's house for a haircut. And then, back at Karen's, Sunday night, Jerry laid out his clothes for court.

"I remember Jerry showing me the suit he was *going* to wear," Lance says now. "He must've gotten it from an older cousin. Big lapels, big collar, pinstripes." Lance smiles. "I said we were going to leave that suit in the past. We were going shopping. We went to a Men's Wearhouse. We got a nice, cream-colored blazer, blue shirt, dark slacks. We made sure we had time to get it fitted right. It wasn't too flashy. It was more conservative, laid-back."

Depending on who you talk to, the caravan from Karen's house to 26th and California that morning was between four and nine cars long, each one packed with members of Jerry's family. His older sister, Desiree. His brothers, Jock and Darren. His aunts, uncles, cousins, all their kids. Bishop Lance Davis, the pastor from Jerry's church. "Being an exoneree," Jerry says, "is a very exceptional situation. I mean, back then, it had only happened 199 times before. How do you do it? How do you survive, make it through to the exoneration? A lot of people don't make it. You got to have the right people, the right support system. I was lucky enough to have that.

"My mind was blank," Jerry says now, thinking about the ride downtown. "Maybe I stopped and changed cars, I don't know. All I really remember is I was trying not to wrinkle my suit. I focused on that. Because when it happened, whatever happened, I didn't want to be in an overwhelmed state."

When the cars arrived at 26th and California, every mainstream media outlet in Chicago was there, waiting for them. Satellite trucks. Reporters. News crews. "We walked in together as a family," says Terri Moore, a younger first cousin. "Maybe thirty of us. Jerry led the way, with this big smile stuck to his face. Then we found out only Jerry was allowed to go into the courtroom, with the lawyers. So we waited outside."

Jerry's court appearance was quick. "People were looking at me. I remember this woman turning to her friend, asking, 'Who is that?' Because things had been set up, arrangements had been made. People knew something important was going on."

Judge Diane Gordon Cannon dismissed Jerry's conviction. When Jerry walked out of court, there was applause from the gallery. In the hall outside, Jerry's family and friends exploded with joyous whoops, high fives, hugs and tears. Now it was time for the big press conference.

Jerry was headed to the pressroom, but somehow—"I was out of my body"—he found himself in a small conference room, where he sat on one side of a ten-foot table with Barry Scheck, Peter Neufeld, Colin Starger and his pastor. On the other side were First Assistant State's Attorney Robert Milan and members of his staff. "I may be forgetting some things," Jerry says now, "in fact, I know I am. But the main thing was I was there with my representatives, and the city of Chicago was there with theirs."

Then, in that small conference room, Robert Milan, on behalf of the State's Attorney's Office, apologized to Jerry Miller. Milan told Jerry that the city of Chicago had been wrong, and, although he had not been around when this injustice occurred, he was truly sorry that it had happened. He offered his deepest regrets.

Marsha Indych, an Innocence Project intern who had worked on the case, saw Jerry right after the apology, before the press conference. "He needed a couple of minutes to decompress," Indych says now, "and we were in this little meeting room. It was such a fraught day. An emotional roller coaster. My heart was bursting. Overwhelmed with joy. But at the same time, there was recognition of how much Jerry had sacrificed, losing time he'd never get back."

This was the first time Indych and Jerry had met in person. A litigator now, Marsha Indych had worked a yearlong internship at the Innocence Project and had been his regular contact throughout the exoneration, updating him, checking in with him weekly. "Seeing him that day, I remember thinking about what a proud man Jerry was, and how pride had been taken away from him. But he never forgot who he was, even when the world treated him in a way that he was not. He was so bright. And he had that special spark. A thing that many people, inside or outside, just don't have. He was indomitable."

There are snapshots of Jerry Miller on exoneration day, and news footage. You can see him, dapper in that cream-colored blazer, a broad smile on his face as he stands in the pressroom, grinning down at the first two rows, every seat filled with Miller family members. Cousin and style guru Lance Lenoir says, "You could see the relief on his face. He proved his innocence, and he got the day he was waiting for so long."

Terri Moore remembers looking up at Jerry on stage as a news reporter, following up on a question, said that Jerry didn't seem bitter. She remembers thinking Jerry's face was going to hurt later, he was smiling so hard. Everyone was, the whole family.

"I dealt with my bitterness," Jerry told that reporter. "And I let it go."

The press conference lasted about thirty minutes,

according to Terri Moore. She remembers the Cook County prosecutor apologizing to Jerry on behalf of the city for what happened. "Jerry just kept smiling the whole time," she adds. "No matter what anyone was saying, Jerry was smiling."

After Milan expressed his regrets for the cameras, he announced that Cook County had also solved the crime. The DNA test that cleared Jerry Miller back on March 28 had given them a hit on the real perp, Robert Weeks, who was in prison on another rape charge. Milan had neglected to mention this earlier, because, according to Barry Scheck, "he wanted to pull focus from our two hundredth exoneration. You know, steal a little thunder. But that's just Cook County, right?"

The next stop for Jerry Miller was the parole office, a few miles away, where Jerry had his ankle bracelet removed. "From far away," Terri Moore remembers, "it must have looked like groups of ants, following each other. There were thirty of us going to the parole board, then, right behind us, all the press. Wherever we went, they followed. And Jerry kept smiling."

The whole group hit Sullivan's for steaks and drinks and celebration. Barry Scheck sat next to Jerry, listening as family members made toasts, and Jerry toasted right back. "I was struck by what a remarkable man Jerry was," Scheck remembers. "He had superb emotional intelligence, but he's not consumed with hatred and bitterness. He's so likeable, so funny, and so winning."

Halfway through lunch, Barry Scheck asked Jerry Miller if he would go back with him to New York on Tuesday morning. The Innocence Project gala, the first one, was Tuesday night, and Scheck wanted Jerry Miller to be there. "It was clear to me that Jerry was a good spokesman for the cause, and he was eager to do it. He had an important story to tell, and I thought he should tell it."

Outside Sullivan's, after the luncheon, Jerry Miller stood with Desiree, his older sister. Desiree looked glum, and Jerry noticed. "I asked her what was wrong," Jerry says now. "She said she couldn't get over what they'd done to me. The cops, the city of Chicago. She couldn't stop thinking about it and really didn't think she could ever get past it."

Jerry Miller laughs, remembering this story. "I told her she *had* to get over it. It happened to *me*. *I* got over it."

Jerry Miller remembers that first trip to New York, the first Innocence Project gala. "I went from a prisoner to hanging out with the movers and shakers," he says. In the weeks after the gala, he would be interviewed by Bill Moyers, appear on the Stephen Colbert show, tell his story of relentless survival, how he made it through. "Life is short," Jerry says now, "and you've got to pick a path. I picked the path that led me home."

Three years after his exoneration, Jerry received a settlement from the city of Chicago for deprivation of his civil rights. He now lives in Virginia and is studying to be a computer programmer. Every day, in all areas of his life, Jerry strives to move forward.

JOHN MANKIEWICZ is a film and television writer whose credits include *The Street*, *The Human Factor* and *The Marshal*. He is an executive producer of the Netflix series *House of Cards*. He is extremely grateful to have met Jerry Miller and believes the Innocence Project is doing God's work.

Editors' Note

The urge to depart from the state that wrongfully convicted and imprisoned them is compelling for many exonerees. Jerry Miller was one of those: After a quarter century of imprisonment for a rape he didn't commit, he left Illinois behind him. He now lives in a beachfront condominium, watches business news shows, exercises and walks on the beach with his fiancée. Although he received a settlement of his civil rights suit, nothing will bring back those long, long years in prison.

Juan Rivera. Photo courtesy of Randy Belice for Northwestern Law

15.

EVERY DAY IS A NEW BEGINNING

LIFE AFTER INNOCENCE

Juan Rivera (Illinois exoneree),
as told to **Laura Caldwell**

———

FREEING AN EXONEREE *is like releasing a newly minted human being onto the planet. For each exoneree, it is like being churned out of a human factory, stamped with a set of looks, a way of talking and then turned out into the world with little or no knowledge of that world or of oneself as a person within it. It's true that upon release any prisoner, guilty or not, who has missed the proliferation of cell phones and myriad other technology will feel left out, adrift. But to an innocent person who has suffered one of the most surreal journeys imaginable, the process of acclimation is intense. Some do better than others. They are experienced practitioners in the art of forgiveness. Most struggle with emotions and anger, but most win that fight on a frequent basis, just like they won the ultimate fight of their life—the one for their freedom.*

Every morning, Juan Rivera wakes before the click.

The click, in prison, was the sound the cell door made when the guards in the station high above you released the bolt on your door at 5 a.m., allowing you to go to the chow hall for a ladle of watery oatmeal. If you didn't take advantage of the open door to your cage, the bolt would soon hammer down again. So even when he wasn't hungry, even when he was deep-bone tired from "sleeping" on a steel bed, Juan Rivera got up. Eventually he awoke before the door opened—waiting, waiting, always waiting to get out.

But he has prevailed. He is no murderer. He is no rapist. He often thought he was losing his mind when they kept saying that he killed a child, a sweet eleven-year-old blonde-haired, green-eyed child. He had thought he might never recover from the jarring, jangling juxtaposition of who they thought he was and who he knew himself to be. But luckily (and he is lucky, he knows this), the court system finally, finally, *finally* agreed with him.

Now that his attorneys have freed him and given him his life after innocence, now that there is no click—no cellies, no lockdowns, no correctional officers—he still wakes before that time. But now he is free to love his fiancée, who loves him and who gave him his miracle baby girl. Another sweet little girl who changed his life.

So he awakes ready to care for his baby, to let her mother get some sleep, but first he must deal with the dread that life has long deposited in his head and in his heart. And the way he deals with it is to ignore, absolutely ignore, it. Once he has acknowledged and moved past that, he blinks his eyes open.

He rolls over and watches his fiancée, her shiny rust-red hair falling past her eyes that he knows are so tired. He wants to take away that tiredness, but a short time later when the baby wakes, crying, she has to nurse her. When his daughter is finally satiated—she can eat so much!—he takes her and burps her. He doesn't like the method of putting the baby over his shoulder; he gets better results by sitting her on his lap, her sternum and neck supported by his large hand and giving a little pat, pat, pat on her back. He can tell when she isn't in the mood for that—he can divine these things because he watches her all day—and so on those mornings, he drapes her lightly on her belly across his knee and once again gives her a pat, pat, pat until the tension in her belly releases. Such small joyful pleasures, those moments.

Then he lifts her, breathing in her delicious baby smell, and cradles her to him, sings to her, bounces her, delights in her. Her first and middle names mean "my light, my little star."

When his little girl is ready to sleep again, he puts her in her mother's arms, and then he dresses for the outside. It's Chicago and so in the summer he need only step into flip-flops. In the winter, so much more is technically required. But in prison, no one gave him coats or socks or scarfs or hats, so now he puts on only the minimally necessary—shoes, pants and two sweaters. Whatever he wears, stepping into it each morning reminds him that he may go outside of his own free will and he may go wherever and do whatever he wants.

And what he wants to do, every morning, is watch the sunrise. How he pined for sunrises when he was in—evidence that the world was still turning.

His apartment is far north of the city, across the street from Lake Michigan, and he walks through only one intersection to reach it. In the summer, the humidity sears; in the winter, gale-force winds pummel him. The lake can be a lapping blue pool one day, then choppy gray and frothy and heaving the next. And although that unpredictability used to sometimes fray the edges of his nerves, he is learning—no, he has learned—to relish it all.

Sometimes he sits on the boulders that rim the beach. Other times he walks to the water's edge. But nearly every day, he thinks of her—the other little girl.

As he watches the fiery-red orb majestically float from the lake, he hopes her twin sister and her family have found a bit of peace. Always he's hit with a wave of grief for them. They don't have their baby girl anymore, their light, their star. But some part of her remains alive in his mind every morning.

Soon he will leave. He will walk—boots clomping or flip-flops slapping—to return to his sleeping fiancée, and also her soon-to-be awaking son, now his son, and he will return to his little girl. His legacy.

> *Juan Rivera was nineteen years old when the police in Waukegan, north of Chicago, began to focus on him as a potential suspect for the 1992 rape and murder of an eleven-year-old babysitter. He was a high school dropout who had recently moved to Waukegan from New York City's South Bronx and had very little guidance at home. His IQ was purportedly low and he had a third-grade reading level. Juan had gotten into some minor trouble, including burglary. He was depressed, got high a lot, and even tried to commit suicide, twice. After being convicted of the burglary, Juan was at home during the murder, wearing an electronic ankle bracelet on a home monitoring system. The system clearly showed he never left his home. After four days of violent interrogation, Juan was forced to sign a confession.*
>
> *He was sentenced to life imprisonment. Numerous appeals resulted, and he was retried two more times. He was reconvicted each time, notwithstanding DNA evidence that ruled him out as the perpetrator, which the prosecution explained away by asserting the eleven-year-old victim had been having consensual sex, something her family and twin denied. Finally, on appeal in 2011, almost twenty years after his initial conviction, the Illinois Appellate Court found that Juan's conviction was unjustified. The prosecution finally dropped the case, and Juan sued Lake County law enforcement for willful miscon-*

duct. Evidence in the civil case showed the prosecution had gone so far as planting the victim's blood on a pair of shoes allegedly owned by Juan but actually not sold in stores until after the crime. Juan received a settlement.

LAURA CALDWELL is the author of fifteen books, including the award-winning Izzy McNeil series, the first of which is *Red Hot Lies*, and the nonfiction work *Long Way Home: A Young Man Lost in the System and the Two Women Who Found Him.* Her research for the latter book motivated her to launch Life After Innocence at Loyola University Chicago School of Law; she continues to serve as its director.

Editors' Note

Although he was imprisoned for eighteen years, Juan Rivera had to endure three separate trials, three separate wrongful convictions for the 1992 rape and murder that he did not commit and from which DNA eventually exonerated him. Juan's case provided ample evidence of misconduct by both law enforcement and prosecutors; eventually, it appeared, the prosecution continued to press its case primarily to cover up such misconduct rather than to incarcerate a guilty individual. In 2011, when the appellate court overturned his third conviction, the court took the unusual step of barring prosecutors from retrying Juan Rivera, and he was released.

THE INNOCENCE NETWORK

The Innocence Network is an affiliation of organizations dedicated to providing pro bono legal and investigative services to individuals seeking to prove innocence of crimes for which they have been convicted. The Network also works to redress the causes of wrongful convictions and to support the exonerated after they are freed.

A directory of the organizations, including contact information, is maintained at www.innocencenetwork .org and can be searched by state or geographical area. The Network's directory also indicates the nature of the cases that each organization serves. For more information, please contact the relevant organization directly.

ACKNOWLEDGMENTS

This book owes its existence to a village of people: Our good friends and longtime agents Amy Moore-Benson and Donald Maass were instrumental in finding a home for the book, and attorneys Ed Klaris and Jonathan Kirsch shepherded us through various contractual, copyright and trademark issues. Megan Beatie and Meryl Moss donated their time as publicists. The Norton people were wonderful to work with: Robert Weil, who loved the project from the beginning and gave us overall advice; Will Menaker and Marie Pantojan, whose editorial hands were steady but sure; Peter Miller, whose publicity ideas and strategic planning were vital; and Mary Austin Speaker, whose beautiful design is evident throughout. Justice David Ellis of the Illinois Appellate Court, an Edgar® Award–winning author himself, was deeply involved with the project. Erin Kresse was the book's original caretaker and creator of www.anatomyofinnocence.com, bringing her years of journalism and editorial expertise to the project. Ashley Stead and Alejandra Barcenas, the Student Directors of Life After Innocence, were key to working with our exonerees. Additional thanks go to all the student members from Life After Innocence, especially Katie Burnett, Jordan Fries, Sarah Patarino, Kathleen Hennessy, Margie Kennedy, Megan Fahey and Carly Cochran. Rob Warden of the Center on Wrongful Convictions graciously donated the Arthur Miller material and offered valuable advice. Of course, we want to express our immense gratitude to each and every one of our writer friends who contributed so much time and effort to bring these astonishing stories to the page and to publicize the book. Finally, we must share our awe and respect for each of the men and women, the exonerees, whose stories are presented here. Their courage shines as a beacon for everyone involved with the book.

BIBLIOGRAPHY

Exonerees Included in This Volume

Gloria Killian

"Gloria Killian." Bluhm Legal Clinic Center on Wrongful Convictions. Accessed October 21, 2016. http://www.law.northwestern.edu/legalclinic/wrongfulconvictions/exonerations/ca/gloria-killian.html.

"Gloria Killian." National Registry of Exonerations. Last modified March 13, 2014. http://www.law.umich.edu/special/exoneration/Pages/casedetail.aspx?caseid=3348.

Judge, Phoebe. "Gloria Killian." The Story. Last modified June 10, 2013. http://www.thestory.org/stories/2013-06/gloria-killian.

Killian, Gloria, and Sandra Kobrin. *Full Circle: A True Story of Murder, Lies and Vindication*. Far Hills, NJ: New Horizon Press, 2012.

Leung, Rebecca. "Wrongfully Accused?" CBS News. Last modified August 26, 2003. http://www.cbsnews.com/news/wrongfully-accused/.

Weinstein, Henry. "Conviction for Murder Reversed." *Los Angeles Times*, March 14, 2002. http://truthinjustice .org/killian.htm.

David Bates

Berlatsky, Noah. "When Chicago Tortured." Last modified December 17, 2014. http://www.theatlantic .com/national/archive/2014/12/chicago-police-torture-jon-burge/383839/.

"David Bates." Bluhm Legal Clinic Center on Wrongful Convictions. Accessed October 21, 2016. http://www.law.northwestern.edu/legalclinic/ wrongfulconvictionsyouth/exonerated/index.html ?details=52.

"David Bates." National Registry of Exonerations. Last modified January 30, 2015. http://www.law .umich.edu/special/exoneration/pages/casedetail .aspx?caseid=4625.

People's Law Office. "Jon Burge, Chicago Police Torture and Justice for Survivors." Accessed October 21, 2016. http://peopleslawoffice.com/issues-and-cases/ chicago-police-torture/.

Ray Towler

"After 30 Years, Jailed Man Exonerated by DNA." *NBC Nightly News* (MSNBC). Last modified May 6, 2010. http://www.nbcnews.com/id/21134540/vp/370 04872#37004872.

Judge, Phoebe, "Ray Towler." The Story. Last modified, June 10, 2013. http://www.thestory.org/stories/2013-06/ray-towler.

"Raymond Towler." Innocence Project. Accessed October 21, 2016. http://www.innocenceproject.org/cases/ray mond-towler/.

"Raymond Towler." National Registry of Exonerations. Last modified December 3, 2014. http://www.law .umich.edu/special/exoneration/Pages/casedetail .aspx?caseid=3696.

Sager, Mike, "The Something You're Not." *Esquire*. Last modified, February 3, 2011. http://www.esquire.com/news-politics/a9457/ray-towler-profile-0311/.

Michael Evans

Coen, Jeff, "Witness in '76 Murder Testifies of Coercion by Cops." *Chicago Tribune*. Last modified July 14, 2006. http://articles.chicagotribune.com/2006-07-14/news/0607140216_1_police-officers-michael-evans-testify.

"Exonerated, Freed, and What Happened Then." *New York Times*. Last modified November 25, 2007. http://www.nytimes.com/interactive/2007/11/25/nyregion/20071125_DNAI_FEATURE.html.

"Freed Man Tells Jury of 27 Years Behind Bars." *Chicago Tribune*. Last modified July 12, 2006. http://articles .chicagotribune.com/2006-07-12/news/0607120254 _1_evans-lawyer-police-officers-key-witness.

Love, James F. "Michael Evans Loses Compensation Lawsuit After 27 Years of Wrongful Imprisonment." *Justice Denied: The Magazine for the Wrongly Convicted.* Last modified Fall 2006. http://justicedenied.org/ issue/issue_34/evans_jd34.pdf.

"Michael Evans." National Registry of Exonerations. Last modified June 2012. http://www.law.umich.edu/special/ exoneration/Pages/casedetail.aspx?caseid=3208.

Mills, Steve, and Jeff Coen. "DNA Tests Gain Release of 2 in '76 Rape, Slaying Freedom Sweet for Men in Prison More than 27 Years." *Chicago Tribune.* Last modified May 24, 2003. http://truthinjustice.org/ evans-terry.htm.

Warden, Rob. "Michael Evans." Bluhm Legal Clinic Center on Wrongful Convictions. Accessed October 21, 2016. http://www.law.northwestern.edu/legalclinic/ wrongfulconvictions/exonerations/il/michael-evans .html.

Ken Wyniemko

"The Innocence Project's First DNA Result—And Its First Exoneration!" *Benchmark: The Thomas M. Cooley Law School Magazine* XXV, no. 3 (2003). Accessed October 21, 2016. http://www.cooley.edu/clinics/_ docs/manexonerated.pdf.

"Kenneth Wyniemko." Innocence Project. Accessed October 21, 2016. http://www.innocenceproject.org/ cases/kenneth-wyniemko/.

"Kenneth Wyniemko." National Registry of Exonerations. Last modified June 2012. http://www.law.umich.edu/special/exoneration/Pages/casedetail.aspx?caseid=3769.

"Ken Wyniemko Interview—The Innocence Project." Innocence Project. Last modified May 9, 2007. https://www.youtube.com/watch?v=B_sQAlIIYiM.

"Ken Wyniemko: Michigan," Innocence Project. Last modified August 26, 2009. http://www.innocenceproject.org/ken-wyniemko-michigan/.

North Shine, Kim. "Freed by Science, He Celebrates." *Detroit Free Press*. Last modified June 18, 2003. http://truthinjustice.org/Wyniemko.htm.

Kirk Bloodsworth

Junkin, Tim. *Bloodsworth: The True Story of the First Death Row Inmate Exonerated by DNA*. Chapel Hill, NC: Algonquin Books of Chapel Hill, 2004.

Audrey Edmunds

"Audrey Edmunds." Bluhm Legal Clinic Center on Wrongful Convictions. http://www.law.northwestern.edu/legalclinic/wrongfulconvictions/exonerations/wi/audrey-edmunds.html.

"Audrey Edmunds." National Registry of Exonerations. June 2012. http://www.law.umich.edu/special/exoneration/Pages/casedetail.aspx?caseid=3201.

Bazelon, Emily. "Shaken-Baby Syndrome Faces New Questions in Court." *New York Times Magazine*.

Last modified February 2, 2011. http://www.nytimes
.com/2011/02/06/magazine/06baby-t.html?pagewanted
=all&_r=0.

"Book Review: *It Happened to Audrey.*" Innocence
Project. Last modified March 08, 2013. http://www
.innocenceproject.org/book-review-it-happened-
to-audrey/.

Edmunds, Audrey, and Jill Wellington. *It Happened to
Audrey: A Terrifying Journey from Loving Mom to Accused
Baby Killer.* Green Bay, WI: TitleTown Publishing, 2012.

Alton Logan

"Alton Logan." National Registry of Exonerations. Last
modified June 2012. http://www.law.umich.edu/
special/exoneration/Pages/casedetail.aspx?caseid=3389.

"Illinois Man Released After Attorneys Reveal Another
Man's Confession." Innocence Project. Last modified April 21, 2008. http://www.innocenceproject
.org/illinois-man-released-after-attorneys-reveal-an-
other-mans-confession/.

"60 Minutes: 26-Year Secret Kept Innocent Man in
Prison." *60 Minutes.* CBS News. Last modified
March 9, 2008. http://www.cbsnews.com/news/
26-year-secret-kept-innocent-man-in-prison/.

Winston, Harold J. "Learning from Alton Logan."
DePaul Journal for Social Science 2, no. 2 (Spring 2009).
Last modified August 18, 2014. http://www.law

.northwestern.edu/law-school-life/studentservices/
orientation/documents/Learning%20from%20
Alton%20Logan.pdf.

Peter Reilly

Barthel, Joan. *A Death in Canaan*. New York: Dutton, 1976.

Boughton, Kathryn, "In the Peter Reilly Case, Odd New Developments." CountyTimes.com. Last modified January 30, 2004. http://www.truthinjustice.org/reilly.htm.

Connery, Donald S. "Peter Reilly's Hard Won Justice." *Hartford Courant*. Last modified September 27, 2013. http://articles.courant.com/2013-09-27/news/hc-op-connery-peter-reilly-murder-case-justice-092-20130927_1_state-police-investigation-barbara-gibbons-new-trial.

Ginny Lefever

"Evidentiary Hearing Request." *LeFever, Virginia, and Heather Reynolds v. Licking County Coroner's Office, Franklin County Coroner's Office, Dr. Robert P. Raker, and Dr. Patrick M. Fardal*. Court of Common Pleas, Licking County Ohio Civil Division. Accessed October 21, 2016. http://www.innocentinmates.org/lefever/Complaint.pdf.

LeFever v. Licking Cty. Coroner's Office. Licking County Ohio Court of Appeals. December 20, 2006. Accessed October

21, 2016. https://cases.justia.com/ohio/fifth-district-court-of-appeals/2006-ohio-6795.pdf?ts=13239 08363.

"Virginia LeFever." National Registry of Exonerations. Last modified September 28, 2014. https://www .law.umich.edu/special/exoneration/Pages/casedetail .aspx?caseid=3378.

William Dillon

Gore, Jeff. "Not Forgiven, Not Forgotten." *Orlando Weekly*. Last modified August 10, 2011. http:// www.orlandoweekly.com/orlando/not-forgiven -not-forgotten/Content?oid=2248116.

Mathis, Kathie. "William Dillon." Innocence Project of Florida. Last modified June 16, 2016. http:// floridainnocence.org/content/?tag=william-dillon.

"William Dillon." National Registry of Exonerations. Last modified June 2012. https://www.law.umich .edu/special/exoneration/Pages/casedetail.aspx? caseid=3177.

Jeff Deskovic

Jeffrey Deskovic. National Registry of Exonerations. Last modified October 24, 2014. https://www.law .umich.edu/special/exoneration/Pages/casedetail .aspx?caseid=3171.

Jeffrey Deskovic Foundation for Justice. Accessed October

21, 2016. http://www.thejeffreydeskovicfoundationfor
justice.org/.

Santos, Fernanda. "DNA Evidence Frees a Man Imprisoned
for Half His Life." *New York Times.* Last modified
September 21, 2006. http://www.nytimes.com/2006
/09/21/nyregion/21dna.html?_r=0.

Walk, Gloria Grening. *Accidental Felon.* Raleigh, NC:
Bialkin Books, 2012.

Antione Day

"Exonoree Diaries: Antione Day." WBEZ 91.5 Chicago.
Last modified September 16, 2013. https://www.wbez
.org/shows/wbez-blogs/exoneree-diaries-antione-da
y/2478776a-3641-461d-b759-77a596cddc48.

Han, Yuri. "Building a Re-entry Home for Exonerees."
Chicago Reporter. Last modified March 23, 2015.
http://chicagoreporter.com/building-a-reentry-
home-for-exonerees/.

"Lee Antione Day." National Registry of Exonerations.
Last modified June 2012. http://www.law.umich.edu/
special/exoneration/Pages/casedetail.aspx?caseid=3162.

Jerry Miller

"Bill Moyers Journal: Jerry Miller." *Bill Moyers Journal.*
PBS. Last modified May 6, 2007. http://www.pbs
.org/moyers/journal/05042007/watch2.html.

"Innocence Project—Jerry Miller." Innocence Project.

Last modified November 13, 2007. https://www
.youtube.com/watch?v=IVnhOtotuEI.

"In 200th DNA Exoneration Nationwide, Jerry Miller
in Chicago Is Proven Innocent 25 Years After
Wrongful Conviction." Innocence Project. Last modified April, 23, 2007. http://www.innocenceproject.
org/in-200th-dna-exoneration-nationwide-jerry-
miller-in-chicago-is-proven-innocent-25-years-after-
wrongful-conviction/.

"Jerry Miller." Innocence Project. Accessed October
21, 2016. http://www.innocenceproject.org/cases/jerry-
miller/.

"Jerry Miller." National Registry of Exonerations. Last
modified June 2012. http://www.law.umich.edu/
special/exoneration/Pages/casedetail.aspx?caseid
=3469.

"Jerry Miller Comes a Long Way Home." Interview.
WBEZ 91.5 Chicago. Last modified July 9, 2007.
https://www.wbez.org/shows/wbez-news/jerry-
miller-comes-a-long-way-home/99c0c936-ada1-
4e4e-8080-dd46eb82d475.

Lydersen, Kari, "Costs Are High for Convictions of
Wrong People." *New York Times*. Last modified June
18, 2011. http://www.nytimes.com/2011/06/19/us/
19cncwrongful.html?pagewanted=all&_moc.semi
tyn.www&_r=2&.

Juan Rivera

Hinkel, Dan, and Steve Mills. "Man Freed After 20 Years in Prison for Waukegan Murder . . ." *Chicago Tribune*. Last modified March 20, 2015. http://www .chicagotribune.com/suburbs/lake-county-news-sun/ crime/ct-rivera-lawsuit-settlement-met-20150320-story .html#page=1.

"Juan Rivera." National Registry of Exonerations. Last modified March 21, 2015. https://www.law .umich.edu/special/exoneration/pages/casedetail .aspx?caseid=3850.

"Juan Rivera Lawsuit: Murder Convictions Reversed, Rivera Sues Lake County Police." *Huffington Post*. Last modified October 31, 2012. http://www.huffingtonpost .com/2012/10/31/juan-rivera-lawsuit-_n_2050854 .html.

Martin, Andrew. "The Prosecution's Case Against DNA." *New York Times Magazine*. Last modified. November 25, 2011. http://www.nytimes.com/2011/11/27/maga zine/dna-evidence-lake-county.html?_r=1&scp=1&sq =%22holly%20staker%22&st=cse.

McDonald, Brent. "The Case of Juan Rivera." *New York Times Magazine*. Last modified November 25, 2011. http://www.nytimes.com/video/magazine/1000 00001180263/the-case-of-juan-rivera.html.

Mills, Steve. "Prosecutor, DNA at Odds." *Chicago Tribune*. Last modified December 15, 2008. http://www.chicagotribune.com/lifestyles/health/chi-081215dna-story.html#page=1.

People of the State of Illinois v. Juan A Rivera, Jr. (Appellate Court of Illinois, Second District, December 9, 2011). Last modified December 9, 2011. http://www.law.northwestern.edu/legalclinic/wrongfulconvictions/exonerations/documents/Outright-Reversal.pdf.

Warden, Rob. "Juan Rivera." Bluhm Legal Clinic Center on Wrongful Convictions. Accessed October 21, 2016. http://www.law.northwestern.edu/legalclinic/wrongfulconvictions/exonerations/il/juan-rivera.html.

Zalman, Marvin, and Julia Carrano. *Wrongful Conviction and Criminal Justice Reform: Making Justice*. New York: Routledge, 2014. https://books.google.com/books?id=VQzfAQAAQBAJ&pg=PA289&lpg=PA289&dq=juan+rivera+exonerate&source=bl&ots=fR_uVTyGAN&sig=2UzVaRBz6zQ1XgqWNS_2oBWMYhc&hl=en&sa=X&ei=868ZVcjWLI-fyAS6sIKwDA&ved=0CD0Q6AEwBTgK#v=onepage&q=juan%20rivera%20exonerate&f=false

Exoneration Issues Generally

Acker, James R., and Allison D. Redlich. *Wrongful Conviction: Law, Science, and Policy.* Durham, NC: Carolina Academic Press, 2011.

Acker, James R., Allison D. Redlich, Robert J. Norris, and Catherine L. Bonventre. *Examining Wrongful Convictions: Stepping Back, Moving Forward.* Durham, NC: Carolina Academic Press, 2014.

Baumgartner, Frank R., Suzanna L. DeBoef, and Amber E. Boydstun. *The Decline of the Death Penalty and the Discovery of Innocence.* Cambridge, UK: Cambridge University Press, 2008.

Benforado, Adam. *Unfair: The New Science of Criminal Injustice.* New York: Crown Publishers, 2015.

Boer, Peter. *Wrongfully Convicted: The Innocent in Canada.* Wetaskiwin, AB: Quagmire Press, 2012.

Brandon, Ruth, and Christie Davies. *Wrongful Imprisonment: Mistaken Convictions and Their Consequences.* London: George Allen and Unwin, 1973.

Brooks, Justin. *Wrongful Convictions: Cases and Materials.* Lake Mary, FL: Vandeplas Publishing, 2014.

Cutler, Brian L., and Steven Penrod. *Mistaken Identification: The Eyewitness, Psychology, and the Law.* New York: Cambridge University Press, 1995.

Doyle, James M. *True Witness: Cops, Courts, Science, and the Battle Against Misidentification.* New York: Palgrave Macmillan, 2005.

Eggers, Dave, and Lola Vollen. *Surviving Justice: America's Wrongfully Convicted and Exonerated.* San Francisco, CA: McSweeney's, 2005.

"Eyewitness Misidentification." Innocence Project. Accessed October 21, 2016. http://www.innocenceproject.org/causes/eyewitness-misidentification/.

Fenton, Reuven. *Stolen Years: Stories of the Wrongfully Imprisoned.* Old Saybrook, CT: Tantor Media Inc., 2015.

Flowers, Alison. *Exoneree Diaries: The Fight for Innocence, Independence, and Identity.* Chicago, IL: Haymarket Books, 2016.

Forst, Brian. *Errors of Justice: Nature, Sources, and Remedies.* Cambridge, UK: Cambridge University Press, 2004.

Gardner, Erle Stanley. *The Court of Last Resort.* New York: W. Sloane, 1952.

Garrett, Brandon L. *Convicting the Innocent: Where Criminal Prosecutions Go Wrong.* Cambridge, MA: Harvard University Press, 2012.

Giannelli, Paul C., and Myrna Raeder, eds. *Achieving Justice: Freeing the Innocent, Convicting the Guilty.* Washington, DC: American Bar Association, 2006.

Gould, Jon B. *The Innocence Commission: Preventing Wrongful Convictions and Restoring the Criminal Justice System.* New York: New York University Press, 2008.

Huff, C. Ronald, and Martin Killias. *Wrongful Conviction: International Perspectives on Miscarriages of Justice.* Philadelphia, PA: Temple University Press, 2010.

Huff, C. Ronald, Arye Rattner, and Edward Sagarin. *Convicted but Innocent: Wrongful Conviction and Public Policy*. Thousand Oaks, CA: Sage Publications, 1996.

Lance, Courtney B., and Nikki D. Pope. *Pruno, Ramen, and a Side of Hope: Stories of Surviving Wrongful Conviction*. Franklin, TN: Post Hill Press, 2015.

Leo, Richard A. *Police Interrogation and American Justice*. Cambridge, MA: Harvard University Press, 2008.

Loftus, Elizabeth F. *Eyewitness Testimony*. Cambridge, MA: Harvard University Press, 1979.

Rabinowitz, Dorothy. *No Crueler Tyrannies: Accusation, False Fitness, and Other Terrors of Our Times*. New York: Free Press, 2003.

Radelet, Michael L., Hugo Adam Bedau, and Constance E. Putnam. *In Spite of Innocence: Erroneous Convictions in Capital Cases*. Boston: Northeastern University Press, 1992.

Scheck, Barry, Peter Neufeld, and Jim Dwyer. *Actual Innocence: When Justice Goes Wrong and How to Make it Right*. New York: New American Library, 2003.

Warden, Rob, and Steven A. Drizin, eds. *True Stories of False Confessions*. Evanston, IL: Northwestern University Press, 2009.

Weinberg, Steve, Neil Gordon, and Brooke Williams. *Harmful Error: Investigating America's Local Prosecutors*. Washington, DC: Center for Public Integrity, 2003.

Westervelt, Saundra Davis, and Kimberly J. Cook. *Life After Death Row: Exonerees' Search for Community and*

Identity. Critical Issues in Crime and Society. New Brunswick, NJ: Rutgers University Press, 2012.

Westervelt, Saundra Davis, and John A. Humphrey, eds. *Wrongly Convicted: Perspectives on Failed Justice.* New Brunswick, NJ: Rutgers University Press, 2001.

For a detailed bibliography of law review articles, magazine articles, books, and other media on wrongful convictions, see http://forejustice.org/biblio/bibliography.htm.

ABOUT THE EDITORS

LAURA CALDWELL is the best-selling author of fourteen novels as well as the acclaimed nonfiction work *Long Way Home: A Young Man Lost in the System and the Two Women Who Found Him.* Her short fiction has appeared in several award-winning anthologies. Caldwell formerly practiced as a civil trial attorney and now is a professor at Loyola University Chicago School of Law.

In 2008, she founded Life After Innocence at Loyola, to aid persons wrongly convicted. Since its founding, Caldwell has served as LAI's director, working with dozens of staff members and law students who advocate for innocent people adversely affected by the criminal justice system, helping them reenter society and enabling them to reclaim their rights as citizens through individualized legal and support services and wider-reaching public policy initiatives. LAI helps them find homes to live in, connects them with jobs, teaches them the basic necessities for functioning in present-day society and assists them in expunging their records and pursuing compensation from the state. LAI is now a model for similar projects around the world.

Caldwell is grateful to the exonerees for having the courage to tell their stories so unflinchingly, and to the writers, who gave of themselves to ensure the book is the best it can be. She also thanks Leslie S. Klinger for his tireless efforts in coediting *Anatomy of Innocence*.

...

LESLIE S. KLINGER is the *New York Times* best-selling editor of the Edgar® Award–winning *The New Annotated Sherlock Holmes* and numerous other annotated books and anthologies. He also coedited, with Laurie R. King, the anthologies *A Study in Sherlock*, the Anthony® Award–winning *In the Company of Sherlock Holmes*, and *Echoes of Sherlock Holmes*.

Klinger formerly served as the SoCal Chapter President and on the National Board of the Mystery Writers of America and is the Treasurer of the Horror Writers Association. He practices tax, estate planning and business law in Los Angeles, where he lives with his wife, dog and three cats.

Born and raised in Chicago, Klinger is a longtime supporter of Loyola University Chicago's Life After Innocence and has volunteered his assistance on tax matters. He was thrilled to be asked by Laura Caldwell to coedit *Anatomy of Innocence* and to have an opportunity to work with her, the amazing individuals whose stories are told in the book and the equally amazing writers who tell them.